# The Toy Book

# The Toy Book

GIL ASAKAWA AND LELAND RUCKER

ALFRED A. KNOPF  NEW YORK 1992

THIS IS A BORZOI BOOK
PUBLISHED BY ALFRED A. KNOPF, INC.

COPYRIGHT © 1991 BY GIL
ASAKAWA AND LELAND RUCKER

ALL RIGHTS RESERVED UNDER
INTERNATIONAL AND PAN-
AMERICAN COPYRIGHT CON-
VENTIONS. PUBLISHED IN THE
UNITED STATES BY ALFRED A.
KNOPF, INC., NEW YORK, AND
SIMULTANEOUSLY IN CANADA BY
RANDOM HOUSE OF CANADA
LIMITED, TORONTO. DISTRIBUTED
BY RANDOM HOUSE, INC.,
NEW YORK.

LIBRARY OF CONGRESS
CATALOGING-IN-PUBLICATION DATA

ASAKAWA, GIL.
THE TOY BOOK / BY GIL ASAKAWA
AND LELAND RUCKER.
P.   CM.
ISBN 0-394-58076-1
1. TOYS—UNITED STATES—HISTORY.
2. BABY BOOM GENERATION—UNITED
STATES. 3. UNITED STATES—SOCIAL LIFE AND
CUSTOMS—1945—1970.
I. RUCKER, LELAND. II. TITLE.
HQ784.T68A83   1991
649'.55—DC20  90-53162 CIP

MANUFACTURED IN
CHINA
FIRST EDITION

# Contents

# The Toy Book

# Introduction

In 1943, the industrial strength of the world's most powerful countries was being flexed in a deadly serious war effort, manufacturing guns, bombs, tanks, planes, and ships. In Philadelphia, a civilian naval engineer working for a shipyard watched as a torsion spring aboard a ship he was inspecting fell off a table and wiggled and bounced back and forth. Amused, he took it home to study. He figured out he could make the spring bounce down stairs and thought he could manufacture one and sell it as a toy.

It took two more years—and the end of the war—before Richard James and his wife, Betty, formed James Industries. When the spring was perfected, it needed a name. Betty James flipped through a dictionary and stopped at a word she thought suited the coiled spring.

Slinky.

Mention the word, and almost everyone holds out his or her hands, palms up, and bounces them up and down, imagining Slinky's back-and-forth motion and the shifting, "slinky" sound—it's one of the best-known toys of the past forty years. Its eighty feet of coiled steel spring jiggles, shuffles, bounces, and stretches back and forth between the hands, and true to Richard James's original hunch, even "walks" down stairsteps, with the momentum of its weight propelling its shiny coils end over end.

Though it's been sold in all sorts of variations, including ones with animal and train shapes attached to its ends, junior sizes, and plastic versions, the basic Slinky has remained virtually unchanged. It's self-contained, easy to manufacture, inexpensive to buy—it sold for $1 when it was introduced, and it still costs only $2.25 today.

Best of all, Slinky is still endlessly fascinating to children and adults alike. It's become a classic toy since its official introduction in November 1945. It's a toy an entire generation—the biggest in the history of the world—grew up with.

That's what this book is about: the playthings of the generation that came after World War II, the memories of hours spent playing with long-forgotten toys. Unlike Slinky, the vast majority of the toys that captured our attention and made it onto our Christmas lists haven't been available for years, and there's already a healthy collectors' market from the last four decades.

But this isn't a book for collectors. There are no lists of all the toys a manufacturer made during the period, no lengthy explanations of a toy's rarity, no price guides. This is a book for people who want to remember the fun they had growing up.

## INTRODUCTION

We devoured our playthings, whether they were related to Howdy Doody or Fred Flintstone, the Rifleman or Illya Kuryakin, the Beatles or the Monkees; we had to have exactly what we wanted, and we wouldn't settle for less. We pestered our parents with our wants, and they were happy to spoil us rotten by granting our every wish.

Our wish lists were compiled from TV commercials, comic books, magazines, and annual Christmas catalogs sent out every fall by the major department stores. We took every Sears, Montgomery Ward, and J. C. Penney catalog and folded the corners of pages with the toys we wanted that year; we circled the items on the pages themselves; sometimes, we cut out the items and posted them on the refrigerator, just in case Mom and Dad forgot.

They didn't dare.

In 1955, for instance, our parents blew $100 million on Davy Crockett toys. After Fess Parker's sentimental portrayal of the pioneer

adventurer appeared on a Disney television show, the country suddenly erupted with frontier capitalism: coonskin caps and buckskins, sweatshirts, sleds, blankets, toothbrushes, lunch buckets, and copies of Old Betsy, Davy's trusty flintlock rifle. Every kid in the country became Davy Crockett.

The pioneer hero wasn't the only TV character to appeal to kids. "The Howdy Doody Show" went on the air in 1947, and by the mid-fifties was one of television's most popular shows—15 million viewers every week, more than Perry Como, Dinah Shore, even Arthur Godfrey. Howdy had more commercial sponsors than today's sports heroes, except he didn't have to wear them on his sleeve.

By 1954, seventy manufacturers were producing Howdy items, including Blue Bonnet margarine, Royal puddings and desserts, Kellogg's cereals, Wonder Bread, Poll Parrot shoes, and Campbell's soups. There were Howdy Doody card and beanbag games, dolls of Howdy, Clarabell, Princess Summer-Fall-Winter-Spring, Chief Thunderthud, Mr. Bluster, and Flub-A-Dub, paint and shovel sets, swim rings, boxed puzzles, sewing kits, and stuffed animals. Six million Howdy comic books were sold a year, and he was featured in Golden Books. RCA Victor records had best-selling Howdy hits.

The toys in this book span the period from the late forties to the early seventies, although it wasn't until the early fifties, when the first kids born after the war were entering grade school, that the toy industry exploded. Before then, the market was limited, and growth was modest. Toy companies, like other businesses, struggled to get by during the Depression, and later most diverted their production to the war effort. In 1940, the toy industry did $84 million in business. By the start of the fifties, the industry was raking in $1.25 billion, and the figures rose dramatically as the birthrate skyrocketed.

It wasn't until after the war that entrepreneurs like Richard and Betty James or companies like Marx, Ideal, Mattel, and Kenner could profit from the vast numbers of children filling the new suburbs forming around the perimeters of American cities.

## INTRODUCTION

The boom of babies peaked in 1957 but continued through 1964, so we've chosen to end the book around 1974, when the last batch of kids was about ten years old and switching on the first wave of electronic games.

Toys can evoke powerful memories. Remember the sound of a Slinky between your hands? Of course you do, as if you'd held one just yesterday. Anyone who's played with Silly Putty and Play-Doh can recall the smell instantly. Binney & Smith, the company that manufactures both Silly Putty and Crayola crayons, found that the waxy smell of Crayolas is one of the twenty most recognizable odors to adult Americans. (The two odors that brought back the sharpest recollections were coffee and peanut butter.)

This isn't a scratch and sniff book, but we've tried to present the toys as they were, through ads, pictures, snapshots from the era. We've dredged up names to jog dim memories: Erector sets, Lincoln Logs, Mr. Machine, Mr. Potato Head, Rock 'Em Sock 'Em Robots, slot cars, electric trains, Betsy Wetsy, Judy Splinters, Easy-Bake Ovens, Spirograph, Silly Putty, Super Balls, Etch A Sketch, Magic "8" Ball, The Game of Life, Bas-Ket, Mouse Trap, Hula Hoops, FRISBEEs, yo-yos, Lightning Bug Glo-Juice, and on and on.

Our playthings were a product of the world we grew up in. Besides providing fun, toys reflected technological advances (look how "science" toys have evolved, from clunky building sets to computer games and Star Wars fantasies); changes in social attitudes (it was no accident that Barbie got a black friend during the height of the civil rights struggle); and values from the adult world (many toys are miniature versions of adult merchandise and help prepare kids to function as grown-ups).

But enough pop sociology. Nobody thought about the cultural implications of an Easy-Baked cake, a three-day Monopoly marathon, or spending the afternoon chasing THRUSH agents around the backyard.

Let's just play.

Fun!

**S**linky may be one of the most familiar toys in the world today, but retailers in the fall of 1945 were reluctant to stock a toy that looked like a refugee from the hardware department. Realizing that Slinky's appeal was in its motion, Richard and Betty James convinced their first retailer, Gimbel Bros., to let them set up a sloping board as a display, giving Slinky the chance to walk its way down to the amazement of shoppers.

They sold their first four hundred Slinkys in an hour and a half. Nobody wanted to buy them just sitting there. But when they were demonstrated, they literally walked away.

Slinkys are still walking away, at a rate of more than two million a year. The family company still manufactures the spring at a plant at Hollidaysburg, Pennsylvania. In 1960, Richard left his family and became a religious missionary in South America, where he remarried and died in 1974. Betty and her six children have run the company ever since.

SLINKY CAME IN MANY VARIATIONS: A SLINK 'EM BOARD GAME; A LONG-POPULAR SLINKY DOG PULL-TOY (YOU DRAGGED IT ALONG, AND THE TAIL END WOULD FALL BEHIND, THEN SUDDENLY PULL UP); A SLINKY TRAIN; SWAMP BUGGY; SEAL; WORM; SLINKY EYES (EYEGLASS FRAMES WITH EYEBALLS BUGGING OUT, WHICH NOWADAYS ARE MASS-PRODUCED AS A CHEAP NOVELTY ITEM).

The Jameses introduced Slinky to the world at an ideal time: in the giddy postwar flush, the economy was booming and so was the population. But in 1945, Richard was still an engineer during the day, and Betty was a housewife with two children to handle in between wrapping, packaging, and driving the toys to retailers. The baby boom was the last thing on the Jameses' minds.

The company these days also sells a few other toys, as well as Slinky variations, including a smaller size and a plastic version. Those plastic Slinkys will remain in the minds of the kids now growing up with them the way the original Slinkys have stayed with the baby boomers.

Thanks to scientific advances made during the war, technology was helping to reshape American lifestyles during the late forties and fifties. And many of the advances made in the name of science were quickly reflected in the toy industry—either with science-based imagery or in the actual creation of a new toy.

Silly Putty, for one, was a by-product of the effort to find a synthetic substitute for rubber. During the war, the Allies suffered a shortage of rubber, requiring strict rationing of products like tires, because the Japanese had cut off access to the world's major rubber-producing regions in Southeast Asia. James Wright, a chemical engineer working for General Electric during World War II, came up with a flesh-colored silicone compound that was close, but not quite rubber.

It bounced when rolled into a ball and stretched like rubber, but snapped when it reached its limits. The compound also was handy for picking up lint and cleaning surfaces like an eraser. Most interesting, it picked up images off

NOT EVEN SLINKY WAS IMMUNE TO COMPETITORS. MR. WIGGLE WAS A SHORT-LIVED MID-FIFTIES KNOCKOFF THAT NEVER CHARMED KIDS THE WAY SLINKY DID.

SILLY PUTTY DID A LOT OF THINGS, BUT IT WAS BEST KNOWN FOR PICKING UP THE FUNNY PAGES AND MAKING THEM EVEN FUNNIER BY STRETCHING THE IMAGE. SILLY PUTTY'S PACKAGE WAS SUBTLE BUT EFFECTIVE MARKETING: IT REMINDED KIDS THAT THEY'D SEEN THE PRODUCT ON TV.

the printed page, such as newspaper photos and panels from comic books. It wasn't the right stuff for General Electric, but Wright was intrigued enough to dub it Gooey Gupp, and create enough to sell it out of a New Haven, Connecticut, toy store.

In a classic example of old-fashioned entrepreneurship, a businessman named Peter Hodgson happened upon Gooey Gupp at the store in 1949 and bought the rights from Wright. Hodgson renamed it Silly Putty, enclosed it in a bright red plastic egg, and sold it through Doubleday bookstores. Silly Putty caught on immediately; Hodgson sold 32 million eggs in five years—not a bad way to start a business. "The real solid liquid," boasted the package the egg came in, which, not surprisingly, was shaped like a TV screen, with illustrations of a boy and a girl looking fondly at the egg.

Silly Putty's still on the shelves today, with only a slight difference in packaging. In 1988, its manufacturer, Binney & Smith, began selling it for the first time ever in green, yellow, and blue eggs as well as the familiar red.

Not introduced until 1965, Wham-O's Super Ball was another toy developed as a result of scientific research. The hard-rubber, high-bouncing ball was created as part of a chemistry experiment with a high-resilience synthetic compound.

The ball took some weird bounces, but it kept going forever. Wham-O licensed the ball and took a year to perfect it before introducing it to the public. When the company unveiled Super Ball, it pulled out all the stops. The balls were manufactured in regular, small, and mini sizes, and Wham-O emphasized its impressive scientific origins with slogans like: "made of new amazing Zectron, four times more bouncy, four times more fun!"

Within a year, competitors had flooded the market with Super Ball clones, and in the spring of 1966 Wham-O felt compelled to announce "the granting of United States Patent #3,241,834 covering the chemical composition of…Super Balls, the products that changed an industry."

Other companies couldn't copy Wham-O's exact Super Ball formula, but that didn't stop them from making inferior, less bouncy versions. Those imitations are still available by the dozens in gumball machines standing outside supermarkets across the country.

Wham-O was accustomed to being a much-copied innovator. The company's Pluto Platter was quietly introduced in 1957. Within a year, Wham-O had renamed the toy FRISBEE. The idea came from the metal pie tins used by the Frisbie Baking Company of Bridgeport, Connecticut, during the earlier

part of the century. Students from nearby Yale University during the Roaring Twenties threw the tins around for fun, and yelled "Frisbie!" to warn passersby.

But those humble origins didn't lead to the Pluto Platter until 1948. Fred Morrison, a California carpenter and building inspector, merged his fascination with flight and a new postwar material, a flexible plastic, and came up with a design for a flying disc that could be aerodynamically controlled with a little wrist action. Wham-O bought the idea and named it the Pluto Platter to capitalize on the country's fascination with space. UFOs were a topic of great discussion in '57, and the toy resembled a flying saucer.

The name was changed to FRISBEE because the public mistook it for a reference to Pluto, the Disney cartoon character. After the switch, the FRISBEE became one of those rare products that can claim total name recognition—virtually all Americans have heard of the FRISBEE, and nine out of ten have played with one sometime in their lives. If your family didn't have one, someone in the neighborhood did.

Along with the many varieties of FRISBEEs that Wham-O produced, the glow-in-the-dark model was ideal for late-night summertime FRISBEE tag games. But the discs weren't all just fun and games; in 1968, the U.S. Navy spent $400,000 to test them as a way to keep flares aloft, shot out of a mechanical launcher.

The toy never made it as a wartime weapon, but FRISBEE throwing did develop into a sanctioned international sport, with world championships and organized competitive meets. There's a section for FRISBEE facts in the *Guinness Book of World Records,* and Wham-O's produced more than 100 million discs over the years.

12

Wham-O was also busy in 1958 with another toy. On a trip to Australia, Wham-O founders Arthur Melin and Richard Knerr saw children using a bamboo hoop during a school exercise routine. The two entrepreneurs thought the hoop idea might catch on with American kids, too. They were right; the Hula Hoop caught on first in Southern California playgrounds and spread like wildfire. The company sold 25 million in four months, and an incredible 100 million within two years.

The Hula Hoop's prototypes were made of wood—ash, the same wood Wham-O used for its famous slingshots (the company's first products in 1948, hence the name)—to imitate the Australian originals. But for mass production they were switched to plastic. During the toy's design stage, Wham-O experimented with other names, including Twirl-A-Hoop and Swing-A-Hoop, before settling on Hula Hoop.

After the hoops were manufactured, the two company founders demonstrated them in playgrounds near their San Gabriel headquarters. If a kid could keep one swirling around him, the men gave it to the kid. The hoops became all the rage. But they really rose to mania stage when a Hula Hoop was featured on "The Dinah Shore Chevy Show"—an early example of telemarketing at work.

In the sixties, Hula Hoop's popularity faded, and other manufacturers who'd jumped on the bandwagon got off. Wham-O kept making them, refining the idea by adding little plastic pellets inside to give the *shoop shoop* sound, and even copyrighting the name and the idea, and the hoop celebrated its thirtieth birthday in 1988.

Some toys that have been around for centuries were updated for the space age. In the late fifties, the Amsco company sold a new variation on tops, the Whizzler; this 79-cent spinning toy made a humming noise that escalated into a high-pitched screech as it went faster and faster. The toy was suspended in the air, and it spun when both ends of its nylon cord were pulled.

In 1971, the idea was reprised by the Kenner Corp. in its Screecher Siren Top. Instead of a string to get it spinning, the Screecher came with a plastic T-Handle Spin-Stick that revved it up. When it got going, it screeched loudly (even kids had to cover their ears), squeezed out sparks, and even launched a twirling triple-bladed "flying saucer."

Another variation on the venerable top, the early sixties MagneTop, featured a conventional top with a powerful magnet built in so it could balance on a wire or a clothes hanger while it spun. The Whee-Lo wasn't quite a top, but its mysterious spinning movement was as entrancing. Its red centerpiece traveled at a deliberate pace along a curved steel wire handle, and it seemed to defy gravity. It never really did anything, but it sure seemed cool at the time.

Later in the sixties, Matchbox, a company better known for its miniature cars, came up with a self-propelling top called the Wizzzer, which had a built-in friction-run motor that you revved up by dragging the top's rubber tip along a smooth surface. Like a gyroscope, the ultimate, scientific top, the Wizzzer balanced on its tip as long as its motor spun with enough revolutions. Unlike the Whizzler, the Screecher, the Whee-Lo, and the MagneTop, the Wizzzer has survived the last two decades, still "the world's wildest whirler," spinning "over 10,000 rpm!!"

Kids didn't have to go for novelty tops, though; manufacturers such as Ohio Art, which made its reputation with metal toys, have always produced lines of more traditional tops.

Another ancient toy that's become a modern favorite is the yo-yo. Like the Hula Hoop, the yo-yo has its origins in South Pacific cultures. In the Philippines, natives used a crude form of the yo-yo, tying a vine around a piece of flint to kill their prey, and retrieving the weapon with the vine. The idea made its way to Europe in the seventeenth and eighteenth centuries, where the yo-yo became a favorite plaything of the French and Spanish ruling classes.

The toy wasn't officially introduced to Americans until the eve of the Great Depression. In 1929, a toymaker named Donald Duncan (who also has the grim distinction of being the man who invented the parking meter) began making wooden

IT SPUN LIKE A TOP, BUT THE WHIZZLER'S ONLY REAL PURPOSE WAS TO MAKE NOISE.

THE GLOW-IN-THE-DARK YO-YO SOLD BY DUNCAN IN THE SIXTIES WASN'T A NEW IDEA. THE COREY GAMES COMPANY CREATED THE GLO-YO OUT OF "LUMINOUS PLASTIC" IN THE LATE FORTIES.

yo-yos, and realizing the power of marketing, hired native Filipinos to demonstrate them to curious department-store crowds.

Yo-yos were a popular fad during the Depression, but the public largely lost interest until 1959, when Duncan contracted with the Flambeau Corporation to manufacture yo-yos out of plastic instead of wood. With the wild, flashy colors and new styles, yo-yos were a hot item again, from the "professional" models to glow-in-the-dark.

During the sixties peak, more than 16 million yo-yos rolled off Duncan's assembly lines a year, but by 1969, when the fad faded again, Flambeau had to buy Duncan out of bankruptcy. Flambeau continues today as Duncan's parent company, and yo-yos have settled down as one of the staples of the toy industry.

In between Duncan's rise and fall and rise again, other companies tried to fill the yo-yo market. In the late forties, Corey Games sold the Glo-Yo. "In the daylight it looks like any other plastic yo-yo. But it isn't like any other plastic yo-yo," the company promised. "IN THE DARK IT GLOWS LIKE A BALL OF FIRE." Unfortunately, the fire faded long before the Glo-Yo could establish itself as a classic.

The latest resurgence of yo-yo interest, thanks in part to the efforts of comedian/musician/entertainer Tommy Smothers, who bills himself as the Yo-Yo Man and does tricks during performances with his brother Dick, has led to companies making handcrafted wooden models again, and even one that claims the title of "The Yo-Yo with a Brain."

What goes 'round comes 'round; kids today are still playing with yo-yos, Hula Hoops, FRISBEES, Slinkys, and Silly Putty.

# Kid Stuff

PLAYSKOOL TOYS HAVE HARDLY CHANGED OVER THE YEARS: THIS CLASSIC LINE INCLUDES THE BRIGHT BLUE AND RED POSTAL STATION SHAPED LIKE A MAILBOX WITH HOLES TO ACCEPT "VARI-SHAPED BLOCKS"; A BAG OF COLORED BLOCKS (SEVENTY PIECES FOR $2.75 IN 1957); A WOODEN COBBLER'S BENCH FOR KIDS TO HAMMER AWAY AT EIGHT "VARI-COLORED PEGS"; A BEAUTIFULLY CRAFTED, FUNCTIONAL TOOL BOX WITH SAFE, MAKE-BELIEVE VERSIONS OF DAD'S TOOLS.

There were a million more babies born in the United States in 1946, the year after World War II ended, than there had been in 1945. Year-by-year birth statistics continued to grow, peaking in 1957, when there were 4.3 million births. By the time the baby boom ended in 1964, 76.5 million American babies had entered the world. That means that every year, more and more newborns were crowding the maternity wards while their two-, three-, and four-year-old brothers and sisters were tearing up their suburban houses looking for toys.

By 1957, the first babies were ten years old and had outgrown several sets of toys. Toy companies were more than happy to keep parents supplied with products for every stage of the children's growth. And companies that aimed toys at infants and preschoolers were the first to profit from the boom.

The population surge was accompanied by more emphasis on toys for young children that would help them develop their imaginations, artistic talents, and the skills necessary to function within an increasingly complicated modern world.

17

The Playskool Institute, a division of a Milwaukee lumber company, was formed in the twenties by two former teachers to manufacture wooden toys for young children. Lucille King, one of the teachers, had used toys—wooden beads, blocks, dollhouses, pegboards, and blackboards, among others—as teaching aids in her classes. By 1935, the Playskool Institute had moved its headquarters to Chicago and was manufacturing forty different toys.

The current Playskool Manufacturing Company was formed during the forties when two of its employees bought the original institute. After several more mergers and acquisitions, Playskool was bought by the giant game manufacturer Milton Bradley in 1968.

The company's most popular toys over the years helped develop children's coordination and visual skills. A 1957 Montgomery Ward catalog said it best: "It's easy to select the right Playskool toy for the right child. Each toy is designed to encourage the mental and physical development of a child according to his age. When you give Playskool toys, you're giving toys that meet high standards of perfection."

Many of Playskool's classic items haven't changed much from their original designs. One of the most basic, wooden building blocks, was added to the line in 1962, when Playskool bought the Halsam Company. Halsam had been started in 1917 by two World War I veterans, Hal Elliott and Sam Goss, who purchased a small woodworking company and began producing blocks, checkers, dominoes, and construction sets. When Halsam bought a competitor in 1955, it became the only American maker of wooden blocks.

Halsam's blocks were truly progressive—edges and corners were rounded for safety, and the brightly embossed letters and numbers were added with nontoxic colors. They even manufactured something they called Hi-Lo Blocks, which featured

PLAYSKOOL'S TYKE BIKES WERE ROLL MODELS FOR LATER TRICYCLES AND BICYCLES.

BY 1957, THE SEARS CHRISTMAS BOOK OFFERED PLENTY OF TOYS FOR TOTS: PARENTS WERE LURED BY THE COLORFUL CONTRAPTIONS, BUT LATER DISCOVERED HOW NOISY THEY ALL WERE.

18

grooved tops and bottoms so children could stack them without having the blocks topple over.

Playskool's history is filled with such farsighted company acquisitions. Holgate Toys of Philadelphia was a woodworking company that had been selling brushes and broom handles since 1789, but during the Depression became known for its innovative toys. About 1930, the daughter of one of the company's principals married educator and child psychologist Lawrence Frank, who pushed for simple toys to be added to the Holgate line. The company hired Jerry Rockwell, brother of the painter Norman Rockwell, to design the toys. Playskool and Holgate merged in 1958, and Rockwell continued to design new products for the company until his retirement in 1971. One of his most enduring creations has been the Playskool Tyke Bike.

Lincoln Logs, one of the most instantly identifiable young children's toys, merged with the Playskool line in 1943. The construction sets evoke visions of early American pioneers, but the inspiration for Lincoln Logs came, oddly enough, from classical Japanese architecture.

The toy was developed by John Lloyd Wright, son of the architect Frank Lloyd Wright, when he accompanied his father to Tokyo in 1916 for the construction of the earthquake-proof Imperial Hotel (a grand building which was later demolished). Frank Lloyd Wright designed the hotel using ancient Japanese wood-joint techniques for its detailing—the Japanese had created such close-fitting overlapping joints that one famous bridge was built without a single nail or other steel device holding it together. The idea intrigued John, who promptly formed the J. L. Wright Co. and began selling Lincoln Logs.

Playskool couldn't corner the market on building toys. One of the first—and most identifiable—construction sets was the Tinkertoy, first introduced in 1914. By the baby-boom years, the tubular Tinkertoy box, with the slogan "world's favorite construction set," was a familiar institution, with new plastic parts added to its colored wooden sticks, connecting pieces, moving parts, and wheels.

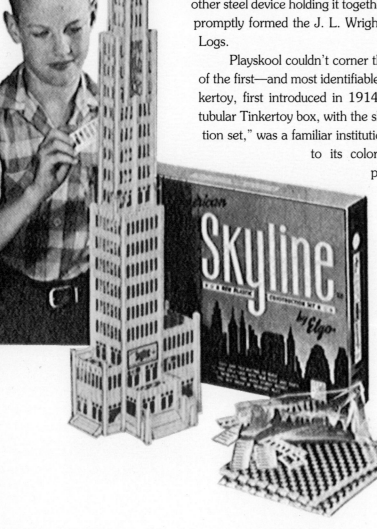

SKYLINE SETS LET BUDDING ARCHITECTS BUILD SCALED-DOWN VERSIONS OF BRIDGES AND SKYSCRAPERS WITH PLASTIC PIECES MOLDED TO LOOK LIKE REAL CONSTRUCTION PARTS.

Kids didn't notice much of a difference; they still screwed up the sets by chewing on the colorful sticks that were Tinkertoys' main building component. It was a good thing the pieces were color-safe.

Other building toys had their heyday, but one toy has continued with its popularity unabated. It's hard to find a building toy that's better loved today than LEGO. The LEGO company was started in the thirties in Denmark by Ole Kirk Chris-

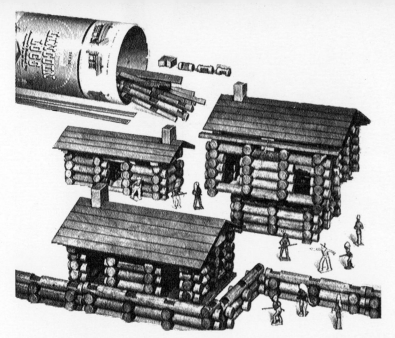

tiansen to manufacture wooden toys; the company grew out of a carpentry shop that fell on hard times during the Depression. Though Lego in Latin translates as "I assemble," the company name came from Christiansen's abbreviation of the Danish phrase *leg godt,* or "play well." The Christiansen family, which still runs the company, expanded its operation after World War II, and bought the machinery and molds to manufacture toys and parts out of plastic.

The first plastic LEGO toy was a fish-shaped baby rattle sold in 1947, followed two years later by a plastic tractor

WITH A LITTLE IMAGINATION, YOU COULD BUILD REALISTIC FORTS, CABINS, STOCKADES, AND HOUSES WITH LINCOLN LOGS. THE BROWN LOGS WITH THE GREEN-SLAT FLAT PIECES (FOR ROOFS, BUT ALSO HANDY AS TABLETOPS—AND PERFECT FOR GNAWING ON, MUCH TO THE CHAGRIN OF PARENTS EVERYWHERE) CAME COMPLETE WITH DESIGN SHEETS IN SIX DIFFERENT-SIZED SETS, WHICH IN 1959 RAN FROM $1 TO $6.

IN THE MID-SIXTIES TINKERTOY MODERNIZED; IT WAS SOLD TO RETAILERS WITH THE ASSURANCE THAT TINKERTOY HAD BEEN UPDATED, REDESIGNED, WITH "NEW, FUNCTIONAL PLASTIC PARTS, NEW DIRECTIONS—SPACE AGE MODELS, AND ADDED PLAY POSSIBILITIES."

that could be assembled and taken apart—an important precursor to LEGO blocks' concept of "additional play value." Also in 1949, LEGO first sold Automatic Binding Bricks, a prototype of what we know today as LEGO bricks—the pieces had the familiar nubs on top, but no tubes underneath. The smaller LEGO System of Play, an integrated set of interlocking pieces with accessories to make all sorts of movable toys and structures, was unveiled in 1955 and further refined in '58 to LEGO's current design, with eight studs on top of the brick and tubes underneath for structural stability. The colorful plastic pieces are sold the world over, and in the United States in more than 120 different sets. According to the company, LEGO sets can be found in half of all American households.

Plenty of less successful building toys are now long forgotten. A late-forties toy called Rig-A-Jig used bright-colored, slotted geometric shapes that snapped together to make all manner of odd-looking creations. The pieces were made of a relatively new compound, "a special,

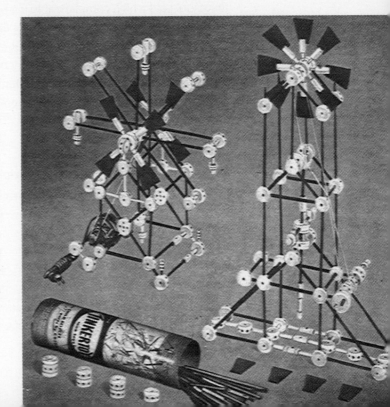

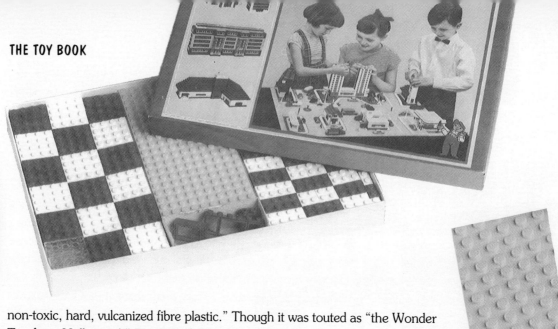

non-toxic, hard, vulcanized fibre plastic." Though it was touted as "the Wonder Toy from Hollywood," Rig-A-Jig faded into toy history.

In the early sixties, Toy Maker was a variation on the Tinkertoy/Lincoln Log concept, using wood and plastic parts to assemble movable toys like boats, cars, buggies, tractors, and wagons. Halsam came out with American Plastic Bricks and Square American Logs, other variations on successful formulas that didn't fare as well as the originals.

And if, as the old saying goes, imitation is the sincerest form of flattery, Playskool paid a high compliment to Tinkertoys by coming up with Makit Toy, a Tinkertoy clone that featured one big difference: connecting balls instead of flat discs. Similar in appearance to diagrams popularized during the dawn of the nuclear age and models of the planets circling the sun, the Makit Toy was sold as "a construction toy for the atomic age child 5 years to 10 years." Playskool eventually paid the highest compliment and took over the manufacture of Tinkertoys.

Some toys were simply aimed at stimulating young kids' artistic abilities and letting them run wild with their imaginations. Ohio Art's Etch A Sketch is the classic toy of this type. It's been modernized, but is still most popular in its original form. Kids through the ages have expressed their creativity by drawing, but it wasn't until 1960 that they had a toy to draw with—even if it took frustrating hours of knob twisting to make smooth curved lines on the shiny silver Magic Screen.

The Ohio Art Company didn't start out with the idea of creating the world's most popular visual-art toy. In fact, the company has a long and illus-

ETCH A SKETCH HASN'T
CHANGED MUCH SINCE ITS
INTRODUCTION. WHEN THE TOY
WAS INVENTED IT WORKED
WITH GLASS PARTICLES
ENCASED BY THE BOX (NOW IT
USES ALUMINUM ONES) THAT
COVERED THE MAGIC SCREEN
WHEN THE TOY WAS SHAKEN;
TWO CONTROL KNOBS MOVED A
STYLUS HORIZONTALLY OR VER-
TICALLY TO ETCH A LINE IN THE
PARTICLES. WITH A LITTLE
PRACTICE, KIDS COULD WILE
AWAY HOURS DRAWING AND
WRITING ON ETCH A SKETCH,
ONLY TO ERASE THE IMAGE
WITH ANOTHER SHAKE. OHIO
ART IMPRESSED PARENTS WITH
THE SPOKESPEOPLE IT HIRED
TO PEDDLE THE SCREENS:
CELEBRITIES LIKE JACK PAAR,
DICK CAVETT, AND A YOUNG
BARBARA WALTERS.

trious history, dating back to 1908, when Henry S. Winzeler, a dentist in Arch-bold, Ohio, sold his practice and started making picture frames. By 1910, Ohio Art's frames were booming—the company eventually sold 50 million frames when the country's population totaled only 92 million.

Ohio Art Company, which moved to Bryan, Ohio, also introduced metal tea sets for young girls in 1920. The Etch A Sketch might be the company's best-known toy, but tea sets are its staple. Over the years, the company's also sold all kinds of stamped steel toys, from cars and boats to globes, pails and shovels, tops, drums, animals, and a still-popular miniature tool chest.

Etch A Sketch Magic Screens were introduced after the company discovered the idea at a German toy fair in 1959 and eventually won the rights to manufacture it. Ohio Art backed Etch A Sketch with the company's first-ever television advertising campaign. With the new generation of youngsters growing like fungus around living rooms lit with the blue flickers of black-and-white TV sets—why do you think Etch A Sketch looks so suspiciously like a TV screen?—the ads worked. The toy was immediately successful, and more than 50 million have been sold since.

For Etch A Sketch's twenty-fifth anniversary in 1985, the company created an executive version, complete with walnut and sterling silver trimmings, and sapphires and a blue topaz atop each drawing knob. The commemorative version sold at a premium: $3,750. The basic Etch A Sketch is still affordable, though. And it's been joined by updated, computerized electronic models to keep up with the times.

Kenner Products' Spirograph is another enduring creative toy. More than 30 million Spirographs have been sold since the toy was introduced in the mid-sixties. The Spirograph's appeal is in its ability to stimulate visual creativity on the part of kids drawing with it, because they can create a million different designs with its combination of gears, wheels, and colored pens.

There's one other possible reason why the Spirograph was so popular from the start: it was introduced during the birth of the psychedelic explosion, when the first baby boom kids were celebrating their growing freedom—sexual, political, and chemical—with the splashy colors and wild patterns of mod-era fashion. And Spirograph patterns, though marketed for younger kids ("ages 5 and up," the box states today, but the ads back then touted its appeal "for all ages"), were nothing if not psychedelic, with their convoluted geometry and eye-popping color effects.

Phosphorescent products were always intriguing to kids—plenty of muggy summer nights were spent capturing lightning bugs in jars—and Kenner managed to capture the glow without the insect. Lightning Bug Glo-Juice, a nontoxic, washable glow-in-the-dark paint, was first introduced in the late sixties.

Other creative toys included crafting materials like old-fashioned clay, and the cleaner, better-packaged Play-Doh, the most enduring of modeling compounds.

Play-Doh was created in 1955 in answer to the needs of a New Jersey nursery school teacher. Joseph McVicker, whose father owned Rainbow Crafts, a Cincinnati company that produced soap and cleaning solutions, was intrigued by his sister-in-law's complaint that her young students needed an alternative to plain modeling clay. The old-fashioned stuff was too hard for tiny hands to do much with, and it dried out. So McVicker came up with a modeling compound with a softer, more pliable consistency and called it Play-Doh.

In 1957, the wife of a Washington, D.C., department store buyer saw Play-Doh demonstrated at an educator's convention and sold the idea to her husband. It was an instant hit—Rainbow Crafts expanded the line to three colors, red, blue, and yellow, in addition to the original grayish white. The company also added a peculiar, vanillalike smell (at least, the company thinks it's vanillalike—most people would simply say Play-Doh smells like Play-Doh).

Other primal toys for aspiring young artists included a series of visually oriented craft sets licensed under "Ding Dong School," the popular preschool and kindergarten TV program which began airing in 1952. On the show, Miss Frances, the matronly teacher, demonstrated projects for kids in between hawking such products as Wheaties cereal with insidi-

PLAY-DOH COULD BE
SQUEEZED, PULLED, AND
FORMED INTO A MYRIAD OF
STRANGE AND EXCITING
CREATIONS. IT WAS A SIM-
PLE, ALMOST PRIMORDIAL
CREATION—NOT FAR
REMOVED FROM MAKING
MUD PIES AND SLOPPY SAND
CASTLES. BEANY AND CECIL,
POPULAR SIXTIES CARTOON
CHARACTERS, HAWKED
PLAY-DOH ON THEIR
PROGRAM.

ous pitches, telling children to make sure their mothers bought Wheaties for them.

In real life, Dr. Frances Horwich was an educator and child psychologist. The Ding Dong School Jumbo Coloring and Cutting Set came with eighteen crayons, a jar of paste, colored paper, scissors, and a picture of Miss Frances—something to treasure. The Ding Dong School Mr. Bumps Set came with wires wrapped in rayon chenille like fancy pipe cleaners, and pieces of Styrofoam to assemble your own oddly shaped figures and party favors. Miss Frances also graced the Official Ding Dong School Fingerpaint and Paintstiks sets.

The ultimate child's drawing utensil, of course, is the Crayola crayon. Other wax crayons come and go, but Crayola is so well known that, like Kleenex, Crayola has become the generic name when someone calls for crayons. The name is a combination of the French word *craie,* for stick of color, and "ola," short for "oleaginous," or oily. The first five-cent boxes of Crayolas were sold in 1903, and they held eight colors. Today, the rainbow has been expanded to seventy-two colors.

The company that manufactured the crayons, Binney & Smith, was formed in 1900 by Edwin Binney and Harold Smith to make carbon black and slate pencils. Binney & Smith's other enduring product is Silly Putty. These days, the company's a subsidiary of greeting-card giant Hallmark Cards, and it manufactures two billion crayons a year.

During the baby-boom years, only two color names were changed. In 1958, "prussian blue" (all Crayola colors are spelled in lower case, even "indi-an red," because tests found that young children read lower case letters more easily) was switched to "midnight blue" after teachers reported that kids didn't know or care about Prussian history. And in 1962, "flesh" was wisely changed to "peach" in response to the burgeoning civil rights movement.

Except for eight flashy, fluorescent colors added to the line in 1972 to reflect the styles of the day, the standard palette wasn't changed until 1990. With great fanfare, Binney & Smith unveiled eight brand-new colors with names such as "cerulean," "jungle green," and "vivid tangerine," and finally retired eight existing colors, including "blue gray," "maize," and "raw umber," for the first time in the company's history.

Even the boxes that Crayolas came in delighted kids, especially the classic sixty-four-color assortment, first introduced in 1958. They were sturdy and designed with a handy flip-top which, with a little imagination and a face drawn on, could be turned into a puppet. The package also included a cleverly integrated sharpener, in which children twirled Crayola nubs for rejuvenation. Unfortunately, the built-in sharpeners left a trail of colorful shavings all over the house.

Another brand name that has dominated the preschool market is Fisher-Price. There are probably very few Americans born since World War II who haven't played with at least one Fisher-Price toy, whether the push-along Corn Popper, Queen Buzzy Bee, Chatter Telephone, or the dozens of clever, noise-making toys that remained virtually unchanged in the Fisher-Price line for decades.

The company was started in 1930, when businessman Herman Fisher teamed up with Irving Price, the mayor of Aurora, New York, and Helen Schelle, a savvy toy store owner, and formed Fisher-Price. The company had humble beginnings, employing a tiny staff to hand-cut wood pieces and assemble them in a converted farmhouse.

From the start, Fisher-Price emphasized toys that would be irresistible to children because they moved and made noises in play.

THE SNOOPY SNIFFER HAD SEVERAL VARIATIONS. IT WAS BORN IN 1938 AS A DALMATIAN, BECAME A BASSET HOUND IN 1958, AND TURNED INTO A BEAGLE IN 1961 UNTIL ITS RETIREMENT IN 1981.

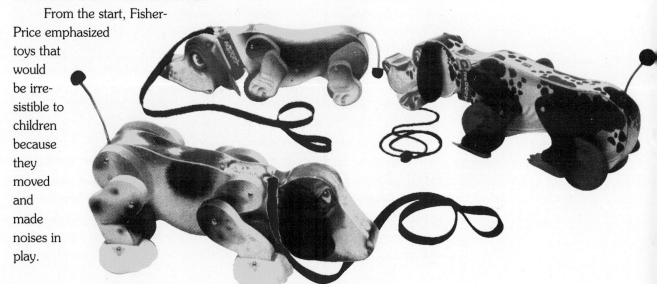

THE BUZZY BEE MANUFACTURED
BY FISHER-PRICE WAS LATER
RENAMED QUEEN BUZZY BEE
AND FITTED WITH A PLASTIC
CROWN; AFTER ONE LAST
MAKEOVER IN 1962, IT
REMAINED UNCHANGED IN THE
FISHER-PRICE CATALOG UNTIL
1985.

The company creed, which still applies, is that its products should have (1) intrinsic play value, (2) ingenuity, (3) strong construction, (4) good value for the money, and (5) action.

Action they had—even an early Fisher-Price stalwart like the Barky Puppy yapped and nodded its head up and down as it was pulled along on its wheels, thanks to a system of simple pulleys and levers. The company's most famous prewar toy was the Snoopy Sniffer, a droll-faced pull-toy with felt ears, rubber paws, wagging tail, and a nose that led the way while the toy made an enchanting *woof woof* sound. Originally introduced in 1938, 4,385,230 Snoopy Sniffers were sold before the toy was finally retired from the line.

In 1946, with a growing sense of consumer euphoria in the air, Fisher-Price announced twenty-six toys in its line, ten of them new designs. It was the first such unveiling in four years. At first, production was still uncertain, because wartime shortages had lingering effects on the economy—inflation doubled the cost of many consumer goods immediately after the war. It didn't help that nagging shortages pinched supplies of certain woods, metals, and rubber. But by '47, the marketplace was much healthier, and the Fisher-Price line sold out for Christmas.

In 1948, with the baby boom firmly under way, Fisher-Price was the leader in its field. The company kept expanding and finding better ways to manufacture its line, at least until the start of the Korean War on June 25, 1950, which held up construction of a new Fisher-Price plant. The Buzzy Bee, a cute little wooden pull-toy critter with an endearing smile, spring antennae, buzzing-sound mechanism, and brightly colored lithographed stripes, came with solid yellow acetate-plastic wings that whirled with every tug.

Plenty of other Fisher-Price designs have been as durable through the years. The Teddy Bear Xilo, first created in 1946, was just one of the many pull-toys that featured a character that beat out melodies on a five-key xylophone, a patented Fisher-Price invention (other xylophone-playing characters included Donald Duck and Mickey Mouse). The same year the Buzzy Bee was put on the market, Fisher-Price debuted its Musical Push Chime, a metal cylinder that looked like a coffee can decorated with nursery rhyme images, with wheels attached to each end. A kid pushed the cylinder along with the detachable wooden pole, and it played a musical melody. To date, the Musical Push Chime is the longest-running toy in the line.

In 1953, Fisher-Price came up with the Space Blazer, one of the company's oddest toys, which reflected the country's growing fascination with all things spaceward (a fascination that would turn into obsession in several years). A spinning flying saucer with the requisite green man from Mars, the Space Blazer featured a bell, rocket engine sound, and a clear plastic cockpit dome.

The 1956 line featured This Little Pig, a string of little squeezable polyethylene porkers that was the first all-plastic toy made by Fisher-Price.

In 1957, the company unveiled three toys still manufactured today: Snap-Lock Beads, the shiny bright plastic beads that fit together and are completely chew-proof against children with baby teeth coming in; the Pull-a-tune Xylophone, a miniature eight-key xylophone complete with drumstick; and the Corn Popper, a simple rolling toy with handle, featuring colored balls that bounce around inside a clear plastic dome.

Fisher-Price's designers still hadn't exhausted their many innovations. The 1959 roster included a Safety School Bus that came with six removable "little people," a concept that led to the successful current line of Little People. That same year, the company came out with its first version of the modern music box, the Jack 'N' Jill TV-Radio. By turning a plastic knob, you could hear a nursery melody plucked out on a real Swiss music box hidden inside, while images of the rhyme rotated by on the tiny TV "screen." One of the last significant new toys introduced during Fisher-Price's

PINKY LEE, A PLAID-SUITED FORMER BURLESQUE COMIC, USED HIS DANCING AND STORYTELLING SKILLS DURING A LONG RUN ON TELEVISION IN THE FIFTIES WITH HIS OWN CHILDREN'S SHOW. HE ALSO WAS A SPOKESMAN FOR EMENEE, PROMOTING COLORFUL XYLOPHONES FOR KIDS.

THE HEZZIE JUNIOR SLIDE WHISTLE WAS SIMPLE AND EASY TO LEARN. ALL YOU DID WAS BLOW INTO THE END AND MOVE THE PLUNGER UP AND DOWN WITH YOUR FINGER LIKE A MINI-TROMBONE. IT WAS GUARANTEED TO DRIVE YOUR MOTHER CRAZY IN TEN MINUTES FLAT.

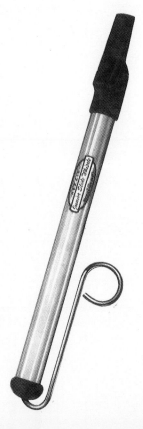

## KID STUFF

glory days was the 1961 Talk Back Telephone, which in 1962 was renamed the Chatter Telephone, another durable idea that still can be found in toy stores today. Right from the start, the Chatter 'phone came with its rolling eyes, plastic receiver, fabric cord, and bell-ringing dial.

In the late sixties, Mattel also had its own, more sophisticated version of the Chatter Telephone called the Mattel-O-Phone. The phone came with small record discs that slid into the base, and you could hear eighteen minutes of conversation with forty different characters, from Snow White and Santa Claus to, of course, Barbie. In its pre-Barbie days, Mattel struggled along by making doll furniture. Ruth and Elliott Handler formed Mattel Creations in the mid-forties with a business partner, Harold Mattson. The company started by manufacturing picture frames (as had Ohio Art, the producer of Etch A Sketch), but branched into doll furniture as a way to use scrap plastic and wood parts. By the late forties, Mattel was also manufacturing a line of musical toys, which became its main products.

Mattel's greatest success with preschool toys, though, is without a doubt its See 'N Say toys. Each of the bright plastic contraptions came with nearly a dozen different images that a pointer could be set at, then the drawstring pulled. Out of a small speaker, a prerecorded voice would approximate the sound that had been chosen (farm animals were always favorites, as well as the Mr. Sound Says series of common noises, like trains, saws, typewriters, and cuckoo clocks). The See 'N Say toys were an enormous hit because of their immediate learning value—once a kid heard the See 'N Say voice intone "Mooo—cow" a few trillion times, he or she never forgot that's the sound a cow makes, even though a real cow sounds somewhat different.

Music was also incorporated into toys. The Hickory Dickory Clock played the well-known nursery rhyme "Hickory, Dickory Dock," while, you guessed it, a mouse ran up the clock. Carnival-styled hurdy-gurdies tinkled out tunes at the turn of a crank. One small metal dog played out "Where oh where has my little dog gone?" when it was cranked up.

COWBOY STAR GENE AUTRY PLAYED A REAL GUITAR WHEN HE SANG WESTERN SONGS AFTER A HARD DAY ON THE PRAIRIE CAPTURING BAD GUYS IN HIS MOVIES, BUT KIDS COULD BUY EMENEE'S FOUR-STRING COWBOY GUITAR, EMBLAZONED WITH HIS NAME.

THE FAB FOUR DIDN'T JUST SELL MILLIONS OF RECORDS; THERE WERE ALSO GUITARS, BANJOS, DRUMS, BONGOS, TRAP SETS, UKULELES, SNEAKERS, BUTTONS, LUNCHBOXES, DIARY BRACELETS, WALLETS, COIN PURSES, JEWELRY, GLASSES, BUBBLE BATH CONTAINERS, AIRLINE CARRYING CASES, CLOTHES, EVEN HALLOWEEN COSTUMES, AND, OF COURSE, WIGS. MILTON BRADLEY EVEN BRIEFLY MARKETED FLIP YOUR WIG, A BOARD GAME PLAYED WITH CARDS, DICE, AND COLOR PICS OF JOHN, PAUL, GEORGE, AND RINGO.

## KID STUFF

Brightly colored Swiss-type Melodé Bells were also popular. They made it easy to ring out melodies by following the color-coded music sheets, just like the wholesome, smiling contestants on "Ted Mack's Original Amateur Hour." Each set had eight bells, one for each tone in the major scale. Another model eliminated the need to pick them up, instead placing the bells in a miniature campanile which was activated by striking a key on the color-coded keyboard.

For many kids growing up in the fifties, their first musical instrument was the chromatic song flute, or tonette. It was a simple instrument, made of plastic with a mouthpiece at one end and small holes designed for the fingers to make the different tones required for a scale, like a primitive clarinet.

Other children's instruments simulated real ones: accordions, guitars, autoharps, harmonicas, and pianos. They were often promoted by familiar stars: Spike Jones, Arthur Godfrey, Gene Autry.

To reach more possible converts, the Jefferson guitar company would often use different colors or perhaps a new name on the same model. One green Jefferson guitar had a By the Sea motif with a couple of happy sailors on a boat; another one was a beach Little Clamdigger. The cowboy version had a horse on it, the Palomino Pony, while another Western version was the Wagon Wheels model. Four dancers adorned the Twist version during the early sixties dance fad, while the Lone Ranger, Silver, and Tonto shared a model.

The guitars were made of enameled cardboard with a cheap wooden neck and a string for a shoulder strap. They were anything but real guitars, but at least they came with a book of chords. Even into the early seventies, there had been little change in the guitars or the advertisements for them. Roy Rogers and Trigger still graced the top of one, while another sported a Hawaiian Holiday motif, complete with hula dancers in grass skirts.

But by the late fifties, a new phenomenon in guitars was being seen. In the wake of rock 'n' roll, Montgomery Ward advertised a "solid-body cutaway electronic guitar," which is, of course, the instrument that changed the course of popular music—the electric guitar.

The music industry didn't take long to catch on to the drawing power of its stars. Rock 'n' roll music was popular with kids, who were eager to buy up anything that helped them identify with Elvis Presley. By the time the Beatles arrived in America in 1964, they were preceded by an arsenal of merchandising material that threatened to swallow them up. As they changed the course of the music world, the Beatles also became the first real rock 'n' roll advertising phenomenon.

WITH THE POPULARITY OF THE LONG-PLAYING RECORD ALBUM STILL ABOUT A DECADE AWAY, MANY FIFTIES PLAYERS WERE ONLY LARGE ENOUGH TO SAFELY SATISFY THE NEW 45 RPM RECORD; LPS HUNG PRECARIOUSLY OVER THE EDGE.

EVEN TRANSISTOR RADIOS WENT MOD, WITH BIZARRE SHAPES AND PSYCHEDELIC COLORS. ROCK 'N' ROLL NEVER LOOKED THIS GOOD.

As the 78 rpm record gave way to the 45, which gave way to the album, children's record players, like stereo systems in general, underwent a complete transformation. A 1947 Pliotone Company all-electric phonograph, although it weighed only six pounds, was bulky-looking and decorated in a stardust motif in royal blue and gold, baby pink and blue, or bright red and gold color combinations. It offered "perfect reproduction" and "exceptional volume" for playing the Mother Goose songs and stories that came along with it.

Radios as well as record players were changing. Fisher-Price was busy stamping out windup music-box versions of toys styled to look like radios, but in the early-sixties heyday of Top 40 AM radio, the electronic transistor revolutionized how kids listened to tunes. In an age where almost everyone owns

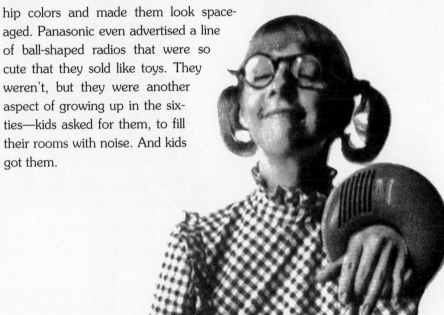

some kind of self-enclosed music playback unit like the Walkman, the tiny transistor radio with its own earphone doesn't seem like much of a modern wonder.

The miniaturized electronic technology, a product of wartime research, was adapted to consumer electronics in 1953, when the first transistor radio, the Regency, was manufactured by Texas Instruments. The tiny $40 radio was sold as a novelty at the time ("the world's smallest radio—small enough to fit in the palm of your hand," said a news report), but it caught on with the public. In three years, sales of portable radios doubled to 3.1 million, and by 1965, the height of the Top 40 era, more than 12 million brightly colored transistor radios with only a tuning dial and volume control (no stereo, no bass or treble) were sold per year.

Transistor radios had classy-sounding names like the Futura and the Medallion and Three Stars. The first made were American brands, such as GE and Admiral, but by the end of the decade Japanese companies like Sony and Panasonic had taken over the market—for good. Thanks to these inexpensive portables, rock music became the ubiquitous soundtrack of the entire generation. Toward the end of the sixties, manufacturers designed transistor radios in hip colors and made them look space-aged. Panasonic even advertised a line of ball-shaped radios that were so cute that they sold like toys. They weren't, but they were another aspect of growing up in the sixties—kids asked for them, to fill their rooms with noise. And kids got them.

# Hello Dolly

**S**ugar and spice and everything nice. That's what little girls were supposed to be made of. And until the women's movement of the late sixties and seventies came along, girls' toys reflected that simple rhyme—with a vengeance.

Girls should play with toys that develop their nurturing instincts, the status quo said—toys like miniature tea sets and cookware so they could pretend to be cooking and serving meals. Baby dolls taught them the all-important lessons of motherhood; "teen" dolls like Barbie were handy role models with their perfect life-styles and safe, bland friends (especially the sexless boyfriend, Ken). Girls could play cowboys and Indians, but only if they dressed up as the sharpshooting Annie Oakley, or better yet, the nonthreatening Dale Evans. Girls who played army with the boys were weird; girls playing baseball, after all, used to be heresy.

One doll that was meant for both boys and girls, though, is the teddy bear. A Brooklyn stationery- and candy-shop owner, Morris Michtom, sometimes sold stuffed toys made by his wife, Rose, by putting them in his window. In 1902, he was inspired by an incident immortalized by a newspaper cartoonist. On a hunting trip, President Theodore Roosevelt refused to shoot a captured bear that had been tied up for him to kill. The cartoonist drew the bear as a helpless cub, and Michtom had his wife fashion a bear cub to put in his shop window, along with the illustration. There were so many requests for "Teddy's bear" that Michtom wrote to Roosevelt and asked if he could mass-produce them, using the president's name. By 1907, the teddy bear had become a familiar doll, and Michtom started the Ideal Toy & Novelty Company.

Stuffed animals have always been a staple of the doll market, but few companies have managed to become identified with specific dolls. Only such names as Gund (a company founded by Adolf Gund in 1898 to make soft toy animals in Connecticut) and Steiff (a German company started by Margarete Steiff after seeing her elephant-shaped pincushions become popular toys) and a few others have become popular brands of stuffed animals. Golden Fleece Toys advertised its stuffed toys during the forties by brand, because they were made with "real lambskin," which made them "So irresistible! So inviting! So tender! It will be love at first sight!"

Raggedy Ann and Andy, rare examples of stuffed human dolls, grew out of the tradition of homemade "rag" dolls, which were popular with families too poor to buy fancy ceramic or wood dolls.

A 1960 article in *Playthings,* the toy industry trade magazine, outlined how a good modern doll should be made, down to the finished tops on socks and the realistic plastic eyes. Though human-looking eyes were a plus, dolls

## HELLO DOLLY

RAGGEDY ANN WAS ORIGINAL-
LY CREATED IN 1914 BY JOHN
AND MYRTLE GRUELLE FOR
THEIR TUBERCULOSIS-
STRICKEN DAUGHTER, MAR-
CELLA. AFTER SHE DIED, JOHN
GRUELLE KEPT HER MEMORY
ALIVE BY WRITING DOWN STO-
RIES ABOUT THE DOLL. THE
STORIES WERE FIRST PUB-
LISHED IN 1918, THE SAME
YEAR THE FIRST MASS-PRO-
DUCED RAGGEDY ANNS
WERE SOLD.

ROSE O'NEILL EXPLAINED
KEWPIE AS "A LITTLE PET
NAME OF CUPID, BUT THERE IS
A DIFFERENCE. CUPID ALWAYS
GETS HIMSELF INTO TROUBLE.
THE KEWPIES ALWAYS GET
THEMSELVES OUT, ALWAYS
SEARCHING FOR WAYS TO
MAKE THE WORLD BETTER
AND FUNNIER."

1. Saran wigs root well, can be washed, combed, and recurled.

2. Superior eyes are made up of several laters of plastic, have "human" look and often feature curling eyelashes.

3. Facial features are doll-like, yet have individual "character."

4. Washable fabrics are important because little girls enjoy being able to wash their doll's clothes.

5. Good material is sheer enough to call for a slip to be worn.

6. Hemming on skirt is sign that attention has been paid to detail.

7. Socks that have a finished top.

8. Real or imitation leather shoes with individual soles.

weren't supposed to be too human: "The facial features," an illustration accompanying the article stated, "are doll-like, yet have individual 'character.' "

Few dolls have had as much identifiable character as Kewpie. In 1911, two years after Rose O'Neill, an illustrator, created a cute little character named Kewpie for *The Ladies' Home Companion,* the Kewpie characters were regulars in the magazines, and there was such a demand for dolls in their likeness that O'Neill finally advertised for someone to bring them to life.

An aspiring sculpture student at Brooklyn's Pratt Institute, Joseph Kallus, answered O'Neill's ad, and crafted a 3-D likeness of Kewpie. The original dolls from Kallus's design were manufactured in Germany and shipped to the United States. In 1925, Kallus started the Cameo Doll company and began making the Kewpies himself. In 1969, Kallus licensed Kewpie to the Strombecker Corporation; it's been passed around since then, to Milton Bradley (Amsco) in the mid-seventies, and to Jesco, Kewpie's current manufacturer, in 1983. Though

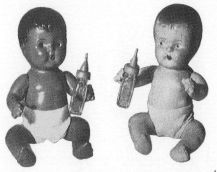

the doll's changed over the years, Kewpie's basic features—the cherubic face with the rosy cheeks and the dangling curl over the forehead—are still very recognizable.

Alongside the ever-popular Kewpies, there were plenty of other dolls for little girls. Some manufacturers switched their assembly lines to overdrive to pump out generic dolls with generic names, which were sold to distributors nationwide without costumes or accessories, so they could be personalized by each company. These "composition" character dolls could be mass-produced in either "white" or "colored" rubber-skinned styles, and came with simple features like moving eyes and "drink and wet" capabilities. It was the first time dolls did things that real babies did.

Toy stores stocked dolls with more personality than these generic figures. Some, like the House of Dolls' Patty Pigtail, were heavily marketed in the late forties, but they're only vaguely remembered now.

In 1946, the Three-in-One Doll Corporation created Trudy, which included a built-in mechanism that caused her to change her expression with a flick of a girl's wrist. "She smiles! (Turn her head) She Sleeps! (Turn her head) She Weeps!" one 1947 ad trumpeted. Her face wasn't very realistic—she looked like a three-dimensional cartoon figure—but at least Trudy was distinctive. A later doll from the early sixties, Tickles, switched back and forth between laughing and crying, depending on how you squeezed her.

Dolls learned to do other tricks: Marybel, "The Doll That Gets Well!," came with unusual accessories, including a cast for her broken arm, and a cast and crutches for her broken leg (from "riding a pony too fast"). She even got chicken pox. And though dolls had been able to "walk" by alternating their leg movement, Toddles was an early-fifties doll that was "the one and only magic muscle walking doll with real leg power." The doll didn't need to be wound up, and her legs weren't spring-loaded.

While some dolls were developing human mobility, others were simply getting more and more human. One of Ideal Corporation's fifties successes ("It's a wonderful doll...it's Ideal!") was Judy Splinters, licensed by Ideal

JACKIE ROBINSON, THE FIRST GREAT BLACK PROFESSIONAL BASEBALL STAR, INSPIRED A DOLL. IT WAS AVAILABLE JUST IN TIME FOR THE START OF BASEBALL SEASON IN 1950.

THE NOMA BRAND'S ACTION TOYS, WALKIES, HAD A FEATURE THE COMPANY CALLED "NEW MECHANICAL SYNCHRONIZA-TION" TO HELP THEM WALK AND ROLL.

# HELLO DOLLY

from the ventriloquist doll of the same name. The doll was created by puppeteer Shirley Dinsdale for the Emmy Award–winning (twice) "Judy Splinters" program of the late forties and early fifties. What made the doll unique was its size—thirty-six inches—and its features, which were proportionate to those of a real four-year-old girl.

Ideal was busy all decade long, inventing new ways to sell girls their dolls. The company came up with such instantly recognizable names as Betsy Wetsy ("Her hair is almost real" crowed the announcer on the commercial, with not a hint of irony—he conveniently forgot to mention that she wet her pants); Little Miss Echo (with a primitive recording device that would repeat back anything you said to it—the idea is still popular today, with the only difference that recording technology has vastly improved); Baby Love 'n Care, the Playtex Dryper Baby (a cross-promotion with Playtex Diapers, which were booming right along with the babies); Tiny Tears, "with rockabye eyes" that slowly closed when you laid her down (pushed through a saturation TV campaign featuring the ventriloquist Shari Lewis and Lambchop, the renowned children's show hosts); a Kissy Doll that puckered her lips ever so cutely with a squeeze; a Bye Bye Baby doll that came with a car seat and waved good-bye; Little Miss Revlon; Rub a Dub Dolly, a waterproof doll that was made to accompany her owner into the tub; and wake-up Thumbelina, a baby doll that opened her eyes and rolled over.

Ideal also licensed and manufactured different sizes of Shirley Temple dolls, from tiny to humongous, which never really looked like the young Shirley Temple, but were hawked by her on ad campaigns anyway. The Shirley Temple dolls were hyped with the same straight-faced silliness as

*Shirley Temple Doll*

Betsy Wetsy: "When you kiss her, her skin feels almost real," claimed the TV commercial, as though that somehow made the doll that much more attractive.

What the doll industry didn't realize was that girls weren't looking for baby dolls with "almost-real" skin. They were looking for a doll that realistically reflected their own image, their own concerns. They found that doll, and her name was Barbie.

In 1959, Barbie was born as a buxom teenager. She was a different kind of doll—girls could go out and buy for her a miniature version of the same black evening dress the socialites were wearing. She was, as Mattel, her creators, called her, a "shapely teenage fashion model," and a serene role model for every girl staring ahead at the trials, tribulations, and ecstasies of life as a teenager.

Barbie's been the center of her own universe ever since. That universe includes friends such as Ken, Midge, and Stacey, but more important, it includes enough wardrobe changes to make Mattel the world's largest producer of women's wear, not to mention one of the great leaders in the toy industry, with more than 500 million dolls sold since 1959.

By that time, the company was adept at finding its market; in 1955 Mattel became a toy industry leader with its pioneering contract to advertise its products on television as a sponsor of the brand-new program "The Mickey Mouse Club." No other toy company had ever invested so much in TV advertising: Mattel signed up for a full year, at $500,000 (just about the company's net worth at the time).

Earlier that year, Mattel had unveiled the first automatic cap pistol, an immediate hit, and the Burp Gun, which wasn't. With the chance to demonstrate the Burp Gun on the air, Mattel turned the initially unpopular toy into a best-seller and set the industry on its ear about the effectiveness of reaching kids directly through TV. The company went on through the rest of the decade coming up with ever more realistic guns modeled after the TV Westerns on which Mattel advertised.

In 1959, Mattel created a whole new market for dolls with Barbie, which was named after Ruth and Elliott Handler's daughter. The couple's daughter inspired Barbie in concept as well as name—the Handlers had noticed she ignored many of her baby dolls for more grown-up interests, like fashion.

At the time, the most popular way to play "grown-up" with dolls was with cut-out paper dolls. But paper dolls' flatness made them unrealistic.

THE ORIGINAL 1959 BARBIE, WITH HER COQUETTISH EYES, SULTRY SMILE—AND BREASTS—WAS THE FIRST SEXY DOLL.

## HELLO DOLLY

As couture fashion designer BillyBoy* points out in his fine—and fun—biography, *Barbie, Her Life and Times,* the original Barbie doll, which featured a vampy, hard-edged, makeup-laden face atop a svelte body, was based on a German line of dolls that already existed called the *Bild* Lilli dolls, fashioned after the racy heroine of a comic strip in the German newspaper *Bild.* Mattel designers started researching a teenaged doll in 1957; the company later bought the rights to the Lilli doll, and Barbie may have been originally made from Lilli's molds.

Toy retailers gave Barbie a cool reception in 1959 when she debuted at the annual Toy Fair in New York, but as she trickled into the stores, the consumer reaction was enthusiastic: the first shipments sold out, and it didn't take any time for American girls to make 11½-inch Barbie their own. Barbie made her debut in the pages of the Sears Christmas catalog in 1961, with a somewhat understated spread amongst all the other dolls of the year. By 1963, Barbie had just about taken over the Sears doll business—eight full pages were devoted to Barbiemania.

Within a few years, Mattel had created an entire fantasy world for Barbie, and even populated it with friends and family members, from the ever-present boyfriend Ken (1961—he arrived with the disingenuous slogan "Ken…He's a Doll") to Barbie's less hip, plain-looking friend Midge (1963, but she exited Barbie's circle of friends in 1967), sister Skipper and her pal Skooter (both 1964), and Skipper's young boyfriend Ricky (the kid, introduced in 1965, was cursed with a vaguely feminine countenance because he was fashioned out of the same mold as Skipper).

The original Barbie, which sold for $3, was touted for her "fashion apparel, authentic in every detail!" "She's curvy and life-like, and she stands alone," an ad proclaimed. That part was certainly true—girls and boys alike marveled at Barbie's well-developed breasts, which caused consternation amongst prudish parents.

Mattel wasn't selling sex appeal, though; it was selling clothes: "Girls of all ages will thrill to the fascination of her miniature wardrobe of fine-fabric fashions: tiny zippers that really zip…coats with luxurious linings…jeweled earrings and necklaces…clothes that really fit. Feminine magic! A veritable fashion show, and every girl can be the star."

But first, every girl had to talk Mom and Dad out of the money to buy all the great stuff for the fashion show. Even at the start, there was an awful lot of up-to-the-minute fashions they had to collect. There were simple cotton dresses, but there was also a Barbie-Q outfit for the great postwar suburban tradition of backyard barbecues (Barbie dressed in a cook's outfit with barbecue

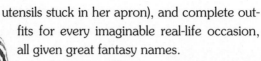

utensils stuck in her apron), and complete outfits for every imaginable real-life occasion,
all given great fantasy names.

There was Sweet
Dreams, a pajama set
that came with a diary,
apple, and alarm clock;
the Picnic Set, with a
checkered shirt, clamdigger
pants, hat, sandals, picnic bas-
ket, pole and tiny plastic fish; the Suburban
Shopper, which had a cotton-and-lace zipper-
backed dress, hat, fruit-filled tote bag, neck-
lace, pumps, and a telephone. One 1965
Skooter package even came with a tiny Barbie
doll, complete with a miniature plastic Barbie carrying case.

Not all the fashions were passing fancies. Barbie has had a decidedly
contemporary work ethic, and she's gone through a slew of professional
careers. Her very first, aside from model and domestic (never a housewife
per se, but she did have a wedding gown set), was as a torch singer in an outfit called Solo in the Spotlight, part of the original Barbie's wardrobe. Since
then, she's been (often in association with Ken) a doctor, nurse, student, student teacher, stewardess for several airlines, majorette, executive, ballet
dancer, and even astronaut.

The couture outfits were based on current fashions (as they still are
today), with a Mattel staffer attending every seasonal show in every fashion

ANY BARBIE ACCESSORY MATTEL
WASN'T INCLINED TO CREATE,
THE COMPANY LICENSED. IN
1962, THE A. J. FRANK CO. MAN-
UFACTURED BARBIE TOILETRIES
LIKE BARBIE BUBBLE BATH,
POWDER MITT, AND COLOGNE,
AND BY 1963, THE IRWIN COM-
PANY WAS SELLING LICENSED
HOT RODS FOR KEN AND SPORTS
CARS FOR BARBIE.

THE BARBIE LINE INCLUDED
ELABORATE SETS WHERE BARBIE
AND HER FRIENDS COULD FROLIC
AT THE BEACH, AT A DANCE, OR
EVEN IN BARBIE'S OWN SUMPTU-
OUSLY APPOINTED EARLY-SIXTIES
CARDBOARD APARTMENT. THERE
WERE LATER DREAM HOUSES, A
CASUAL PATIO FURNITURE SET,
AND A THEATER (WITH CORRE-
SPONDING COSTUME SETS FOR
GUINEVERE AND KING ARTHUR,
CINDERELLA AND THE PRINCE,
RED RIDING HOOD AND THE
WOLF, AND BARBIE AND KEN
ARABIAN NIGHTS).

center of the world, studying, absorbing and copying all the major designers' styles. The attention to detail paid off: Barbie outfits' craftsmanship was as realistic as could be managed on an eleven-inch doll, and details down to cuffs and linings were exact. Even the fabrics were top-notch, with silk jacket linings, and every innovation in synthetic fabric fitted doll-size. It's no wonder why Barbie was so popular with the girls—they lived out their fashion fantasies with Barbie and her friends.

Mattel never got complacent about Barbie's popularity. The company improved the doll every chance it got, starting with a facial makeover within a couple of years that softened Barbie's looks and took out the hard, arched eyebrows and heavily mascaraed visage left over from her German ancestry. There were subtle changes, too. Barbie in 1959 came with hoop earrings, which were replaced by pearl by the next year and discarded altogether by 1965. With different plastics, her color became more natural over the years. Her hair's also been changed, from silky to various Saran plastic styles. During the early sixties, she helped popularize the bubble cut, a cousin of the bouffant, with a demure version that suited her fast-paced life-style.

IDEAL TRIED TO WOO BARBIE OWNERS WITH TAMMY CRUISING IN HER ROADSTER.

In 1964, Barbie's eyes blinked; in 1965, the line was upgraded with bendable legs that made living out adult fantasies even more realistic. Girls could also buy a Fashion Queen Barbie that came with three different wigs, cut in the bubble cut, pageboy, and flip—all popular styles of the mid-sixties. Later in the decade, Barbie and her friends learned to talk, with the help of a pull cord that switched on a mechanism with prerecorded messages.

Barbie was also available during 1967's Summer of Love with "twist 'n turn waist—pose her any way you want!" Aside from bendable legs, the dolls at the time came with "real eyelashes." In 1970, Mattel created Living Barbie, a whole new line that made the dolls more posable, more realistic than ever before.

Barbie's evolution also included some exotic features: In 1965, Color Magic Barbie could change the color of her hair or outfits by brushing on a clear, nonstaining solution. The Color Magic Fashion Designer Set came with three separate outfits that needed no sewing (you could attach flocking, glitter, or floral patterns which were all adhesive-backed), and a molded dress form to do all your handiwork on, just like the mannequins real dress designers used.

There were more friends, too. When fashions went "mod" in the mid-sixties as a result of the Carnaby Street craze, it was decided that Barbie's image didn't suit much of the wild plastic, psychedelic clothes from across the Atlantic. So Mattel naturally created a British friend for Barbie, Francie, who wore all the latest groovy threads and fab fashions. Francie was also joined by raven-haired Casey, another British character, and then the first Barbie doll based on a real person, a miniature version of the high-fashion queen of the times, Twiggy. Also during the mod era, Barbie and Skipper got little (6 3/8" high) twin siblings: a sister named Tutti and a brother named Todd.

Other characters came and went: P.J., who arrived on the shelves dressed in an orange and pink flower-print miniskirt, pink lace panties, love beads, and mod sunglasses; Christie, the first black doll in Barbieland, whose arrival was a reflection of the social changes under way; Truly Scrumptious, a character from the movie *Chitty Chitty Bang Bang;* and Julia, another black doll, based on the TV character played by Diahann Carroll. In the 1970s, Talking Brad was the first black male doll in Barbie's clique; later in the seventies, Mattel also produced two more celebrity Barbies, Donny and Marie Osmond.

Over the years, Barbie's face has been molded into a pert, cute smile, instead of the vaguely slutty countenance of the original 1959 Barbie. When she was born, Barbie looked European; during the sixties, she looked like an East Coast sophisticate (Jackie Kennedy was definitely an inspiration). In 1967, she was given a makeover that transplanted her to the West Coast look, with softer features that reflected a schoolgirl innocence, and long, straight hair. Her wardrobe also got an updating, and to encourage girls to throw their lot in with the new Barbie look instead of the old (the trendier clothes didn't suit the pre-1967 Barbie, which had been tailored for classy evening wear and a mainstream, suburban "look"), Mattel came up with an unprecedented trade-in program, offering the new Barbie for $1.50 in exchange for the old Barbie. The tactic worked—1.2 million dolls were turned in to retailers in one month.

In the seventies, she settled into what she looks like today: a doe-eyed, perky West Coast valley girl. Still, she continues to serve as a model for fashion-conscious girls the world over, with more than twenty million Barbie outfits sold every year.

The numbers didn't escape other doll manufacturers. Many other companies got into the teenage doll business to augment the sales of the still popular baby dolls. One of the most aggressively promoted was American Character's

## HELLO DOLLY

Tressy doll, which came with her own world of accessories to match Barbie's opulence. Though her fashion standards somehow never quite matched Barbie's, it wasn't for lack of trying.

Tressy did have one novel feature on Barbie, though. When Tressy was introduced in 1964, American Character made a nod to Barbie in the evolution of dolls. A brochure acknowledged "teen model dolls with life-like figures and high fashion clothes," but proclaimed, "Then … came Tressy … a teen model doll with a life-like figure, high fashion clothes—and HAIR THAT REALLY GROWS!"

American Character didn't let up on Barbie clones; after Tressy, the company created Dawn, a swinging, hip teen doll that could fit right in with Barbie's British friends. Dawn also came with the usual array of glittering accessories, growing hair, and friends. Like the late-sixties Barbies, Dawn had swiveling hips and bendable legs, all the better to twist, frug, and groove away on the dance floor. You could even buy a go-go dance floor set, Dawn's Disco, to which Dawn and her friend Kevin could be attached—the two danced gleefully, mechanically twisting away, long hair swirling to the beat. Like Barbie, she was as realistic as American Character could make her. Dancing Dawn moved her legs and hips when you moved her arms up and down.

The TV commercial for Dancing Dawn cryptically appealed to prurient salaciousness, thanks to her wild, psychedelic outfit, complete with miniskirt and fringed jacket: "You'll love to dance with Dawn," the commercial announced, "and Dad will, too!" It was as if the manufacturer was appealing to Dad's lecherousness to get him to buy Dawn for his daughter.

For more respectable entertainment, though, she and her friends could be lined up on an elaborate stage for a fashion show, where the dolls walked out, down the runway, swiveled, and returned backstage. And while it seems logical that girls would get bored staging the same fashion show over and over, it didn't stop the manufacturer from grinding out such fantasy spreads.

The Ideal Corporation chased after Barbie sales, too, with Tammy, a teenaged doll that had girlish features. With her round, bulbous head and coquettish eyes, she wasn't as believable a teenager as Barbie or even Tressy. Ideal backed Tammy with the usual arsenal of accessories, though, including her very own MGB sports car. Made of "unbreakable polyethylene" in fash-

TRESSY'S MAIN ATTRACTION WAS A FEATURE THAT CONTROLLED THE LENGTH OF HER HAIR: SQUEEZE A BUTTON AND YANK IT LONGER, OR TURN THE BUTTON AND PULL IT BACK INTO HER HEAD. SHE CAME EQUIPPED WITH CURLERS, PINS, VARIOUS HAIR-SETTING SOLUTIONS, BRUSHES, AND COMBS. LIKE BARBIE, TRESSY HAD A FULL LINE OF ACCESSORIES, INCLUDING A FURNISHED APARTMENT WITH A PENTHOUSE PATIO, A COMPLETE CARDBOARD BEAUTY SALON, AND TRESSY'S HAT BOUTIQUE, STOCKED WITH AN ENVIABLE SUPPLY OF HATS.

ionable turquoise, the car, along with the doll to drive it, were pushed, according to Ideal's own trade ad, "on network and spot TV week after week, all through the year." Ideal also covered its bases with Crissy, whose deep red hair grew at the touch of a button.

Even less-known manufacturers got into the post-Barbie frenzy. Valentine Dolls was busy promoting its Hug-A-Bye Baby dolls on TV, but it also started to push its Twisteens line of swivel-hipped action dolls, with the endorsement of twisting superstar Chubby Checker. Mattel answered the dance craze with its Swingy doll, a battery-powered young girl that danced feverishly, or walked with vigor.

Barbie may have been inspired by high-fashion paper dolls, but she didn't replace paper dolls entirely. Well into the mid-sixties, Merry Manufacturing, the company best known for its Miss Merry line of make-believe cosmetics, sold an array of paper dolls, in characters from the familiar (Donna Reed, Bride of Franken-stein) to the generic (Kim, Toni, Jo) and the goofy (Miss Merry herself, a precocious cartoonlike little girl). The flat dolls came with storybooks to add to the enjoyment of covering the cutouts with the vinyl "Rub 'n Stay" clothes that peeled off again and again.

Not all dolls in the sixties were modeled after Barbie and her teenaged pals. In 1963 Ideal came out with a cuddly Pebbles doll, based on the popular weekly cartoon series "The Flintstones." Mattel also kept up its stock outside the ever-expanding world of Barbie. The company created Cheerful Tearful, the latest in a long line of baby dolls that drank from a bottle and used the water to perform other realistic actions.

Mattel didn't stop there. Girls could choose Baby First Step, which walked or roller-skated with lifelike steps. Baby Secret whispered prerecorded messages in your ear, and her lips moved

CHUBBY CHECKER TOOK THE TWISTEENS TO THE DISCOTHEQUE, WHERE THEY COULD SHOW OFF THEIR SWIVELING HIPS.

GIRLS COULD BUY RECORD DISCS THAT INSERTED INTO CHARMIN' CHATTY AND MAKE HER SAY HUNDREDS OF CUTE PHRASES. HER BOOKISH LOOKS GAVE HOPE TO NERDY GIRLS EVERYWHERE.

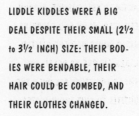

LIDDLE KIDDLES WERE A BIG DEAL DESPITE THEIR SMALL (2½ to 3½ INCH) SIZE: THEIR BODIES WERE BENDABLE, THEIR HAIR COULD BE COMBED, AND THEIR CLOTHES CHANGED.

when she spoke. Baby Teenietalk also had moving lips, but her messages were spoken in the broken English of a child just learning to speak. Chatty Cathy, a very popular late fifties/early sixties talking little girl (twenty inches tall) doll that repeated eighteen different phrases like "I love you" and "Where are we going?" was updated in the late sixties into Charmin' Chatty.

Also from the mid-sixties era, De Luxe Reading Corp. offered a slightly generic doll called Suzy Cute, which had the requisite drink-and-wet feature, but which also raised her arms when her tummy was pressed. Shindana Toys created Baby Nancy, a black infant doll, in 1968.

In the seventies, infant dolls made a comeback after years of taking a backseat to teen dolls. Kenner's Baby Alive, for instance, was the best-selling doll of 1973. Baby Alive was advertised as "the closest thing to a real baby that any doll could be. Her mouth moves as she eats or drinks from the bottle. When she is fed, her spoon or bottle nipple activates the real lifelike mouth or swallowing action. When the spoon is removed, Baby Alive chews and swallows for a few seconds more. She drinks like a real baby… bubbles even form in her bottle when she drinks."

As the sixties dragged into the seventies, another trend started: dolls began shrinking. Baby dolls were still being manufactured, and the Barbie-led teen assault was in charge of the market. A still open field was tiny dolls. Mattel, as usual, was right in the fray with such high-visibility (thanks to endless barrages of TV advertising) creations as Liddle Kiddles, cute, big-eyed dollettes with rooted hair and miniature accessories, and Skediddle Kiddles, the same thumb-sized

IDEAL'S PEBBLES DOLL WAS INTRODUCED IN 1963, A FEW MONTHS AFTER THE FLINT-STONES' BABY DAUGHTER JOINED THE TV FAMILY.

# SPARKLE

PAPER DOLLS SURVIVED INTO THE PSYCHEDELIC ERA, THANKS TO KENNER'S FASHION FUN SPARKLE PAINTS SET. SANDY SPARKLE WAS A TWO-DIMENSIONAL TEENAGER THAT GIRLS COULD COVER UP WITH A MOD WARDROBE OF "10 UP-TO-DATE FASHIONS." KENNER ADDED ZIP TO THE CONCEPT WITH TEN "JEWEL-LIKE SPARKLE PAINTS WITH JEWEL-LIKE NAMES SUCH AS AMETHYST, GARNET, ZIRCON, EMERALD, RUBY AND SAPPHIRE." GIRLS COULD DAB THE GLITTER-LADEN COLORS AS DETAIL, OR SMEAR THE STUFF ALL OVER THE OUTFITS TO SUIT THEIR TASTES.

dolls with an attachment that made their legs "walk" as you pushed them along. Mattel also introduced Baby Small-Talk and Sister Small-Talk, which were tiny dolls that spoke.

The king of miniature dolls, however, was undisputably Uneeda, a manufacturer which had been making dolls since 1917. The company became best known for its odd-looking troll dolls, which were ugly, but popular for their four-inch-tall goofiness. By the late sixties, Uneeda sold variations of troll dolls with electric-colored hair (the trolls' highlight) under such silly names as Groovees, Wishniks, Peewees, and Heehees. (A new series of troll dolls started up again in the eighties.) The company also got sidetracked into a bizarre assortment of Pixie Petal People, which were "Tiny dolls that live in flowers and play with you in the daytime hours." Oh, well, you can't read the market for toys accurately all the time. Every company has had its share of flops—it's only the lucky ones, like the Ideals, Mattels, and Uneedas of the world, that can afford to blow a few and

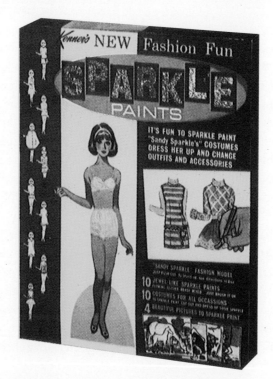

### HELLO DOLLY

come back with other, more exciting ideas.

And those companies and more worked hard throughout the fifties and sixties to enchant the millions of young girls on their way to womanhood with every possible doll idea. When dolls weren't enough, they turned to entertaining the girls directly with toys that appealed to what were then the values that they supposedly aspired to: home, hearth, and motherhood.

Girl Crazy

**I**f girls were to grow up to be complacent little homemakers, society had to train them to aspire to little else from an early age. Girls, alas, like their mothers, were stuck at home. Mom had babies, girls had dolls.

Most dolls weren't part of a mass-marketed world of accessories the way Barbie was. But if some manufacturers hadn't realized how much extra profit could be made from brand-name accessories for their dolls, other companies were happy to supply generic products to suit all dolls.

Mattel began its long, successful run in the toy industry by making doll furniture, so that might explain the company's all-encompassing strategy with Barbie. But owners of other dolls had to rely on companies such as Amsco (short for American Metal Specialties Corp.) for items like a plastic Doll-E-Bath, Doll-E-Crib, and Doll-E-Youthbed, or the Doll-E-Swing. All were just like the real thing, only scaled down for a girl's dolls.

Another manufacturer had the foresight to match the real-life population explosion with doll furniture, selling a bunk bed "for busy 'Little Mothers' with more than one 'child' and limited space in the nursery." Amsco even had eighteen-, twenty-six-, and thirty-inch high chairs and a thirty-inch "pottychair" in 1950, just in time for the first wave of baby-boom girls reaching four and five years old.

"Now for the first time, little mother can train her wetting doll properly," an ad for the Doll-E-Pottychair proudly proclaimed.

Two decades later, Amsco was still at it, except the company was catering more to the profitable post-Barbie teen doll market with a line of Mini Appliances that included a realistic refrigerator, sink, stove, washer, dryer, and dishwasher. The miniature appliances had shiny enamel finishes, smoked plastic see-through doors, and tiny groceries and kitchenware.

Amsco didn't stop with furniture and appliances, either. The company pushed its all-steel doll-sized cookware sets, including the Doll-E-Nurser, a complete old-fashioned bottle kit. The Nurser included a "blue enamel pot and lid, rustproof bottle rack, 6 bottles, 6 rubber nipples, nipple jar and lid, plastic funnel and measuring spoon, measuring cup and bottle brush"—most of which girls today wouldn't know what to do with, thanks to simple formulas and microwaves.

In the late sixties, Amsco had modernized its technology to match the times. The Wonder Sterilizer, modeled after contemporary nursing sterilizers, was a sleek appliance that came with four "milk" bottles. When a girl added water, it made "boiling" noises until the milk was "sterilized," without the benefit of batteries. Of course, girls could skip the cumbersome sterilizing process altogether, because Amsco was the company that manufactured the amazing Magic Bottle, which appeared to be full of milk that trickled away when it was tilted upside down.

If you got bored with playing "little mother" to a brood of crying, drinking, and wetting dolls, you could scale down the experience and play with dollhouses, which have been around almost as long as dolls. At the height of the baby boom, dollhouses were mass-produced by such companies as Happi Time, Marx, and T. Cohn.

For around $5, department stores offered a fine suburban layout with a lithographed steel facade that came off to reveal the treasures of homemaking. Happi Time's thirty-eight-inch-high, forty-five-piece dollhouse had a realistic floor plan with a staircase leading to the two-bedroom upstairs; one was nicely appointed in pink plastic furniture for the baby girl in the family. It had all

MORE THAN 10 MILLION MAGIC BOTTLES HAD BEEN SOLD WHEN AMSCO ADDED A NEW FEATURE AND RENAMED IT CRY BABY MAGIC BOTTLE. THE NEW, IMPROVED VERSION EMITTED A CRYING NOISE DURING THE "FEEDING" AND STOPPED WHEN THE BOTTLE "EMPTIED."

MINIATURE DOLLHOUSES—DECORATED IN THE CURRENT STYLE AND FURNISHED WITH IMMACULATE, IF MIDDLE-CLASS, TASTE—ALLOWED GIRLS TO PLAY HOUSEWIFE AS WELL AS JUST MOTHER. IF NOT YOUR OWN, YOU KNEW A FRIEND OR RELATIVE WHO HAD A TWO-STORY SPREAD WITH THREE BEDROOMS AND A SEPARATE GAME ROOM, COMPLETE WITH PING-PONG TABLE AND PIANO.

the requisite middle-American appliances that postwar economy made afford-able, such as a console television set and a washer and dryer. The toilet seat even flipped up. The dollhouse also had a working front door equipped with a real doorbell and a switch that actually flooded the front room with light. One of Marx's popular sellers in the mid-fifties was a realistic T-shaped ranch house—again, it was a style becoming more and more familiar in the booming suburbs. A dollhouse-sized grocery store was also available for shopping trips.

These miniaturized 'burbs were peopled by families of three- or four-inch stiff plastic figures (at least, Dad was that tall; other members were "propor-tionately sized") that unfortunately weren't remotely realistic. Some of the fancier brands, like one 89-cent family of four sold in the late fifties, were at least jointed at the waist, knees, and shoulders. Marx's dollhouses came with "four vinyl children." In 1956, the company even sold an astounding fourteen-piece doll family for 95 cents that included a mother and father, a kitten, and eleven children! For large-scale play, not necessarily with large-sized families, girls could also buy individual rooms, like a $15 bedroom set for eight-inch dolls (unlike those of all the TV couples during the fifties, the dolls' bedroom had only one bed with two dressers).

Girls didn't always need dolls to play grown-up: there were some women's vocations that weren't tied to motherhood, after all—although women would of course give up those jobs if they had a child.

There has always been the respectable medical profession, where women's nurturing instincts could serve mankind unselfishly. Doctor's kits for

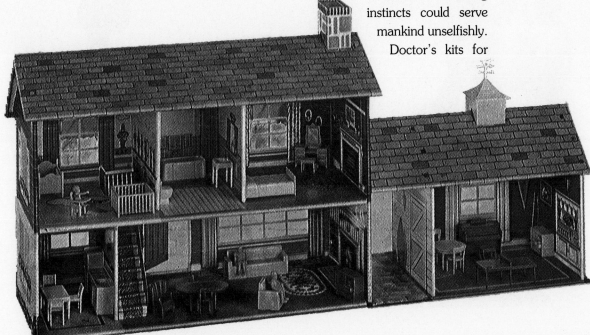

boys and nurse's kits for girls have been staples of the toy industry for decades. Few were as complete and realistic as Amsco's early-fifties gems, Kidd-E-Doctor and Kidd-E-Nurse kits.

Girls could also aspire to be professional decorators. The Irwin Corporation tried to encourage that pursuit with its *House & Garden*–endorsed Interior Decorator Set, which offered "1000 and 1 interchangeable combinations of colored pieces of furniture, floors, walls, rugs and even plumbing fixtures in a miniature home."

Still, toys for girls always came back home, with play versions of all of Mom's household goods. Play tea sets were a staple of girlhood, though they cultivated a sense of gentility that most girls unfortunately never achieved in adulthood (how many girls grow up to host tea parties?). Ohio Art stamped out its first colorfully lithographed metal tea sets in 1918. The company

THE TOM THUMB TYPEWRITER AND CASH REGISTER FROM 1952 WERE CALLED "EDUCATIONAL TOYS," BUT THEY WERE CLEARLY MEANT FOR SECRETARIES- AND CASHIERS-TO-BE.

BRUMBERGER, A LONGTIME MANUFACTURER OF PLASTIC MOLDED PLAY TOYS, SOLD ITS POPULAR SWITCHBOARD PHONES WELL INTO THE MID-SIXTIES, THOUGH THE TOY WAS DESIGNED LONG BEFORE THE AGE OF SLIMLINE AND PRINCESS MODELS.

THE KIDD-E-DOCTOR AND NURSE SETS CAME WITH OFFICIAL-LOOKING BLACK SATCHELS CONTAINING TWO LIFT-OUT TRAYS, FILLED WITH "64 *GENUINE* MEDICAL PRODUCTS AND AUTHENTIC-LOOKING REPRODUCTIONS OF PROFESSIONAL INSTRUMENTS AND ACCESSORIES ... EVERYTHING TO SATISFY THE LONGING OF A BOY OR GIRL TO PLAY DOCTOR OR NURSE." BOTH KITS (WHICH WERE IDENTICAL EXCEPT FOR THE "DOCTOR'S DIPLOMA") SOLD FOR A MERE $1.98 EACH.

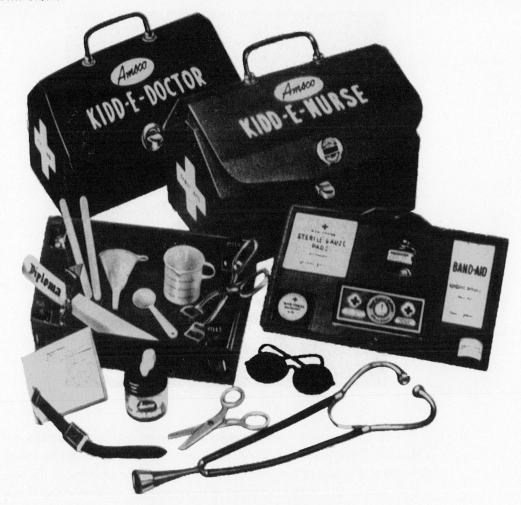

still manufactures tea sets today, but they're now plastic miniatures of Pfaltz-graff ceramicware—appropriate for today's upscale young girls.

Plenty of other manufacturers packaged tea sets for girls. Aluminum, an increasingly popular material in the postwar years because of its light weight and ease of manufacturing, became the standard for pots and pans.

Scaled-down versions of adult kitchen goods are still a solid part of the toy market. Chilton's early seventies Qualitea Sets included plastic versions of the durable Corning Ware cookware Mom used (even a Corning Ware–styled fondue set), as well as plain tea sets and various aluminum cookware sets. Mirro, a real-life aluminum cookware company, cashed in on girls' make-believe needs with its own line of toy pots and pans, called "mother's miniatures."

THE MOST IMPORTANT THING
ABOUT TEA PARTIES WAS SET-
TING THEM UP. ONCE EVERY-
THING WAS IN ITS PLACE, YOU
DIDN'T NEED TEA OR SNACKS,
AND YOUR GUESTS WERE OFTEN
DOLLS AND STUFFED ANIMALS
FROM THE CLOSET.

Play versions of household items expanded beyond simple utensils and cookware. Small appliances like toasters were easy to reproduce in scaled-down versions, though few companies could match the detailing of the late-sixties Amsco line, which included a Wonder Perk coffeepot that made percolating sounds without batteries or winding ("Works On Scientific Principle!" the box told the girls, though it never explained what principle that might be), and the Wonder Corn Popper that—you guessed it—popped over and over again, without batteries or winding.

The luckiest (or wealthiest) girls could convince their parents to buy them miniature appliances as detailed as Gabriel-Nassau's Little Miss Nassau appli-

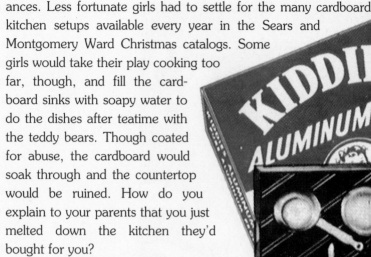

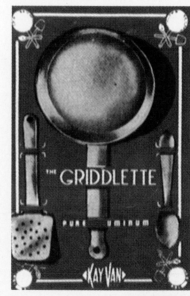

ances. Less fortunate girls had to settle for the many cardboard kitchen setups available every year in the Sears and Montgomery Ward Christmas catalogs. Some girls would take their play cooking too far, though, and fill the cardboard sinks with soapy water to do the dishes after teatime with the teddy bears. Though coated for abuse, the cardboard would soak through and the countertop would be ruined. How do you explain to your parents that you just melted down the kitchen they'd bought for you?

It was much easier to explain that you'd ruined a cake you were trying to bake. In 1962, Kenner Products introduced the Easy-Bake Oven, a miniature appliance with a twist—it really baked cakes and cookies, using ordinary light bulbs for a heating source.

The Easy-Bake Oven was a smash because it upped the ante on make-believe. Now, girls didn't just imagine they were cooking in their play kitchens—in conjunction with the prepackaged Betty Crocker mixes available for the oven, the ads for the Easy-Bake insisted that it made "Food As Good as Mom's." The Easy-Bake's still going strong today, though its shape has been modernized to look like a microwave oven.

Kenner was started by three brothers, Al, Phil, and Joe Steiner, in Cincinnati, Ohio, in 1947, debuting with the Bubbl-Matic Gun, and distributing a wide variety of toys through the decades. Along with Mattel, Kenner was a pioneer in advertising its products on TV; the company was an early sponsor of Captain Kangaroo.

THE EASY-BAKE OVEN COULD WHIP
UP ANYTHING THAT MOM COULD,
BUT NOBODY POINTED OUT IN THE
SATURATION-TV AD CAMPAIGNS
THAT THE CAKES WERE THE SIZE OF
A HOCKEY PUCK, AND JUST ABOUT
AS APPEALING.

GIRL-SIZED LITTLE MISS NASSAU
APPLIANCES WERE MADE OF
HEAVY-DUTY STEEL FINISHED IN
TYPICALLY SIXTIES "GLEAMING
TURQUOISE ENAMEL." THE STOVE,
OVEN, SINK, FRIDGE, AND CABINET
CONNECTED TOGETHER WITH A
"CHANNEL-SLIDE" ASSEMBLY THAT
MADE IT EASY TO MAKE A COM-
PLETE KITCHEN IN MINUTES .

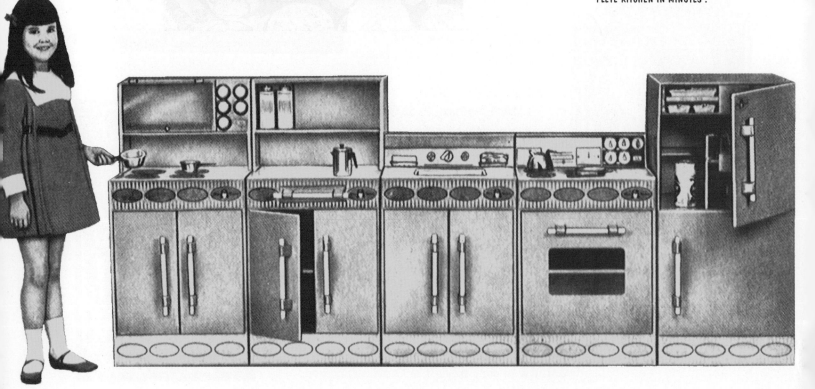

## GIRL CRAZY

"SWEET POTATOES IN THE PAN,
UNCLE JACK WILL EAT 'EM LIKE A
MAN," WENT THE OLD SAYING.
NOBODY MENTIONED THAT GIRLS
WOULD HAVE TO COOK THE POTA-
TOES IN THEIR MINIATURE POTS
AND PANS.

TOY MANUFACTURERS KNEW TO
REACH A CHILD'S SPENDING
POWER THROUGH HIS OR HER
SWEET TOOTH. THE FREEZE
QUEEN DAIRY STAND MACHINE
MADE SOFT ICE CREAM WITHOUT
HAVING TO CRUSH ICE OR TURN
WEARISOME HANDLES.

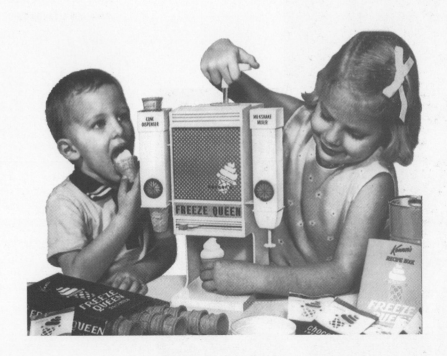

AMSCO HOOKED UP WITH NAME-BRAND MAKERS OF ADULT HOUSEHOLD EQUIPMENT, SUCH AS BISSELL, TO COME UP WITH THE LITTLE QUEEN BISSELL SWEEPER AND SWEEPER SET, WHICH CAME WITH HELPFUL EXTRAS LIKE A BROOM, DUST MOP, AND DUSTPAN.

NORSTAR OFFERED A MULTITUDE OF WORK-AS-PLAY ITEMS, "PACKED IN ALL PRICE RANGES," INCLUDING A LITTLE NORSTAR SWEEPER, BABY PACKAGES OF BRILLO PADS AND BAB-O CLEANSER, THE USUAL ARRAY OF SHORT BROOMS AND MOPS, AND A MASSIVE BOXED SET OF EVERYTHING THAT MOTHER'S LITTLE HELPER COULD POSSIBLY NEED, THE NORSTAR LITTLE HANDI-AID CLEANING SET.

60

### GIRL CRAZY

By the late sixties, Kenner knew it had a good idea on its hands. The company came up with a surprising array of working kid stuff. The Big Burger Grill could cook hamburgers with one light bulb. The only drawback was that it was painfully slow compared to Dad's backyard charcoal grill—it took five minutes to serve up a small pancake, and more than ten minutes to cook a marginally respectable burger. The Whiz Fizz soda fountain made "over 50 bubbly sodas...in 3 delicious flavors." Suspiciously like Fizzies, the once-popular tablet that made a carbonated soft drink when dropped in water, the Kenner Whiz Fizz dispensed a premeasured amount of flavored powder activated by water from the fountain.

Kenner attracted plenty of competition with its use-'em-for-real appliances. Chilton licensed a Kool-Aid dispenser that looked like the water coolers at Dad's office, as well as a 7-Up fountain that looked just like the one at the movie theater. Hasbro always had its longtime favorite, the Frosty Sno-Cone Maker, which got dragged out every summer to augment corner lemonade sales.

Mattel, which had been enormously successful for a couple of years with its various Incredible Edibles novelty gadgets, entered the almost normal world of cake baking with its Kooky Kakes.

GIRLS COULD HOLD THEIR OWN BAKE SALES WITH PINT-SIZED CAKE AND COOKIE MIXES, AND EVERY UTENSIL THEY NEEDED.

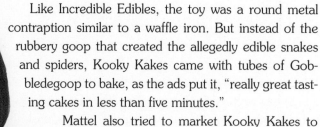

Like Incredible Edibles, the toy was a round metal contraption similar to a waffle iron. But instead of the rubbery goop that created the allegedly edible snakes and spiders, Kooky Kakes came with tubes of Gobbledegoop to bake, as the ads put it, "really great tasting cakes in less than five minutes."

Mattel also tried to market Kooky Kakes to both boys and girls. "Even more incredible, it's going to be as big with boys as it is with girls," the trade ads insisted. "Boys love the fun of making the silliest, craziest-looking cakes ever. Girls love the fun of making cakes just as beautiful as they want."

And, just to make sure retailers got excited about Kooky Kakes in 1968, Mattel assured them that "millions of boys and girls are going to be seeing this new toy on television."

Also on TV with commercials about the same time, Junior Chef was busy matching Kenner's research and development staff with all sorts of working home appliances. The Poppity Popper made tiny servings of popcorn that somehow managed to appear huge on TV. Junior Chef also made a miraculous home version of something that was only a luxury at carnivals and circuses, a kids' version of the Cotton Candy Machine. The company even went one-on-one with the Easy-Bake Oven with its See It Bake Oven, and later, its Junior Chef Tasty Custard Maker. Much to Junior Chef's credit, the company's advertising usually showed both boys and girls cooking away on its various working toys.

When it came to upholding long-standing sexual stereotypes, few companies could match Topper. The company created some of the most macho of boys' war toys (the Johnny Seven One Man Army gun was a clear harbinger of Rambo), but it cemented the image of girls' domesticity with its simple, memorable line of kitchen appliances: Suzy Homemaker. The line, introduced in 1966, centered on a Super Oven that could actually bake bigger cakes than the Easy-Bake. It extended beyond the predictable goods and sold a Sweet Shops set to make your own candy (the TV commercial was backed by a not-so-subliminal bubblegum-rock musical track). By the late sixties, the line was reintroduced with all-new color schemes. The commercials urged shoppers to

THE GLAMOUR NAILS PACKAGE FEATURED TWO SETS OF PLASTIC SLIP-ON FINGERNAILS FOR GIRLS TO PAINT TO THEIR HEARTS' CONTENT.

PLAYING GROWN-UP FOR GIRLS MEANT HAVING PLAY MAKEUP. FOR TEN CENTS, A GIRL COULD GET TWO STYLISH TUBES OF LIPSTICK CANDY, ONE FOR AFTERNOON AND ONE FOR EVENING. THE INGREDIENTS WERE SUGAR, CORN SYRUP, AND "U.S. CERTIFIED PURE FOOD COLORS."

THE BUFFY MAKE-UP AND HAIRSTYLING SET SAVED MOTHERS THE SHOCK OF SEEING STRANGE FASHION DISASTERS ON THEIR CHILDREN, BECAUSE THEY COULD EXPERIMENT WITH BUFFY'S FACE. "SAFE NON-TOXIC, WASHABLE COSMETICS MAKE GROWN-UP OR WAY-OUT MAKE-UP EFFECTS EVEN A MOTHER CAN LOVE," AN AD ASSURED.

stick to Suzy Homemaker because, "Now your young homemaker can do her own thing," surrounded by the psychedelic colors of her choice. And when the cooking was done, manufacturers were ready to help girls clean up after themselves with miniature mops, brooms, and appliances.

When the housework was done and the baby dolls put to bed, girls could settle down to the business of being, well, girls. That meant toy companies could make a profit on their primping.

When they were young, that meant harmless play cosmetics made of plastic, or the late-fifties phenomenon, Candy Lipstick.

Merry Manufacturing's Miss Merry line of cosmetics and accessories was one of the most recognizable brand names. In 1962, Miss Merry sets included make-believe fantasy, but also some touches of reality. The Beauty Sleep kit came with "jars of make-believe bedtime and beauty creams, hand lotion, Curity cotton balls, Gayla bobby pins, miniature towel, styling comb." The Play Bath not only had "play bubble bath," it also came with "two bottles of real shampoo, tray of three miniature bars of real soap." For aspiring young vamps, Miss Merry's Model's Make-up was a "Brand new outfit for tiny glamour girls! Novel trapezoid-shaped box holds make-believe lipstick, liquid rouge, three eye shadows and eyebrow pencils—all safe, of course."

And just for good measure, a Mister Merry Play Lighter set appealed to boys with its "little man outfit supreme." The set came with Philip Morris bubble gum cigarettes and a plastic lighter, which flipped open to reveal a flashlight bulb for a flame.

One of the biggest glamour markets for adult women is hair care, so it's no wonder that toy companies paid close attention to trends that could translate into products for girls. In 1968, while teenaged girls were letting their hair grow long and heading for hippie enclaves, Kenner was pushing its Easy Curls kits to their younger sisters, so they could style their hair "just like Mom!" In fact, Kenner was sure that Easy Curl and its illustrated booklet with all the latest styles would be effective, and the company crowed that "Mom will want it, too!"

By 1970, Amsco had introduced wigs for girls to try on far-out new styles without the hassles of curling or ironing their tresses. The next year, Amsco created an entire Girls World line (the company had been bought by Milton Bradley), and was selling a flip wig that could be easily colored red or brown and then shampooed back to blond.

The same year, Girls World offered a Buffy Make-Up and Hairstyling Set featuring the head and hair of Buffy Davis, the girl played by Anissa Jones in the hit TV series "Family Affair."

If girls got bored getting all made up with no place to go, they could always turn to artistic pursuits. They could develop their abilities with Jon

ARTIST JON GNAGY SOLD HIS "LEARN TO DRAW" SETS THROUGH TELEVISION.

## GIRL CRAZY

Gnagy's drawing courses, or skip the skill and try paint-by-number. Or they could turn to Lisbeth Whiting's dazzling array of projects. The company offered crafts, such as the dolls you could make with yarn.

No boy would be caught dead snipping away at yarn to make a rag doll, but he might get interested in making tile ashtrays. Lisbeth Whiting thought so, anyway—the hard craft kits (as opposed to the soft, knitting-based kits) like the ashtray, Mosaic Tile Candy Dish, and Lazy Susan, as well as the Fun With Sticks box (five "exciting" things you could make with Popsicle sticks!) show both boys and girls hard at work, er, play, crafting to their heart's delight.

Lisbeth Whiting probably had it wrong, though—in 1962, boys were ready to shoot to kill.

65

HAVE GUN WILL TRAVEL

WIRE PALADIN
SAN FRANCISCO

A GAME BASED ON THE TV PROGRAM

# The Big Bang Theory

**W**hile girls played Suzy Homemaker with their dolls and appliances, boys were more likely than not out in the woods having the time of their lives, playing out pseudo-violent fantasies such as cowboys and Indians, GIs and Jerries, cops and robbers, or spies and counterspies.

What red-blooded American boy could forget the thrill of his first gun-and-holster set? The pistols gleaming inside their see-through box? Strapping those leg ties on and tilting your felt hat with the roll-up brim and rayon chin strap just the way Rowdy Yates wore his? The unforgettable smell of spent caps, embossed cowhide, and nickel plate as you looked in the mirror to make sure you looked just right?

The fifties and early sixties were the great age of the television Western, a time when there was a nightly video diet of bottles broken over heads, "aw, shucks" romantic encounters between girls in long dresses and men with hand-

kerchiefs around their necks, and showdowns in front of the flimsy buildings along Main Street, Texas, the Kansas plains, or the Arizona desert.

Western movies had been popular since the twenties, when Tom Mix, Hoot Gibson, William S. Hart and the boys rewrote the history of the taming of the American West in big-screen black-and-white. It was only fitting that these myths should be distilled into half-hour drama/comedy television bits by the fifties.

The first Western heroes on television were crossovers from movies or radio—children's heroes like Hopalong Cassidy, Roy Rogers, the Lone Ranger, the Cisco Kid, and Gene Autry. But by the mid-fifties television was putting its own mark on the Western; by 1959 there were more than thirty different Western series on the tube. And though they were aimed at adult audiences, many had commercial endorsement tie-ins with toys.

Some were unforgettable. Richard Boone was Wire Paladin, the moody troubleshooter who smoked 58-cent cigars and quoted the English romantic poets. More important for the kids, he took his enemies out with a big, black Colt .44 whenever necessary in "Have Gun Will Travel." Steve McQueen's bounty hunter, Josh Randall, wore his sawed-off carbine in a holster and used it like a pistol in "Wanted: Dead or Alive." Yancy Derringer, in the show of the same name, was portrayed by Jock Mahoney, who used the genteel tiny one-shot pistol he was named after. And a Disney show based on a character named Texas John Slaughter, played by author-to-be Thomas Tryon, had to pull his pistol crossways from the left side, but he could still outdraw any opponent.

But the biggest Western character of the decade didn't star in a long-running series. The Davy Crockett craze of 1955 spawned a mini-industry. And it gave birth to one of the most unusual toys ever: the

EVEN THE WESTERN CANINE HERO RIN TIN TIN HAD A GAME NAMED IN HIS HONOR. "THE ADVENTURES OF RIN TIN TIN" AIRED FROM 1954 TO 1959, AND FEATURED THE GERMAN SHEPHERD AND OLD WEST CAVALRY SOLDIERS LT. RIP MASTERS AND RUSTY.

STANDARD EQUIPMENT FOR ALL YOUNG COWPOKES INCLUDED THE RIGHT HAT, A TRUSTY GUN, AND A BOUNCING BRONCO.

coonskin cap. The coonskin cap and everything else that went with Davy Crockett represented the first baby-boomer fad.

And it all started so innocently. In October of '54, Walt Disney Studios announced it was producing a TV program called "Disney-land," a one-hour weekly series offering wholesome family entertainment. It would have the same spirit as Disneyland, the theme park opened just the year before in Anaheim, California. That December the program aired the first of what would be only three segments featuring the adventures of frontier hero Davy Crockett.

Within seven months, seventeen versions of the segment's theme song had been recorded, and sales of coonskin caps went through the roof. In fact, the wholesale price of raccoon tails went up from 25 cents per pound to $8! American kids wanted so badly to become Davy Crockett that toy companies happily obliged with more than $100 million worth of rubber knives, flintlock guns, lunch boxes, tablets, comic books, bows and arrows, moccasins, costumes, and on and on.

Davy Crockett mania stopped overnight. By late 1955, the newly acknowledged buying bloc of kids, the first wave of whom were pushing ten years old, were already looking for the Next Big Thing.

There were plenty of candidates. Chuck Connors twirled his .44-40 Winchester rifle like a baton as Lucas McCain in "The Rifleman." Johnny Yuma, played by Nick Adams, was a shell-shocked, disenfranchised angry Civil War casualty who sported a sawed-off scattergun and a postwar trauma chip on his shoulder in "The Rebel." And perhaps the most unorthodox hero was Earl Holliman's Sundance Kid in "Hotel de Paree." Holliman didn't need his gun; rather he blinded his opponents with the silver discs that made up his hatband.

There were all these and more heroic role models for boys of the Eisenhower era to emulate. Dapper Hugh O'Brien was "brave, courageous, and strong" in "The Life and Times of Wyatt Earp." He sported a longer-barreled Buntline special, 50-cap repeater. You could be Sugarfoot, Sheriff Clay Hollister of "Tombstone Territory," Hoss or Little Joe Cartwright on "Bonanza," Johnny Ringo, Stoney Burke, Sgt. Preston of the Yukon, the Virginian, Marshal Dan Troop, Wild Bill Hickok, or, later, Jim West ("Wild Wild West"), each in pursuit of the ever-present bad guys. You could ride the Wells Fargo wagons with Dale Robertson, be a Texas Ranger like Hoby Gilman, patrol the streets of Dodge City as Marshal Matt Dillon, or make fun of Westerns in general like James Garner's Brett Maverick.

Though they all killed and wounded many a baddie, there was never any blood shed on those TV Westerns—just as with the toy guns the kids were packing. And there were plenty of guns, forged in the image of the Western stars, for the kids to pack.

As with other childhood heroes, Roy Rogers merchandise was all-encompassing. There were outfits for young Roys and Dale Evanses (it was rare to acknowledge that girls also played Western) in all colors. The Roy Rogers phone, a walkie-talkie setup with several hundred feet of wire, was available, as Roy reminded in the TV ad, so you can call down to the bunkhouse and check on the ranch hands. Roy never tried to justify the fact that the Old West wasn't tamed by a network of phone lines. Tiny figurines were created of all the characters: Trigger, Dale's horse, Buttermilk, Pat Brady and his jeep, and Bullet the German shepherd, plus the Roy Rogers Fix-It Chuckwagon.

You could dress like your favorite star, with Western-style embroidered shirts and pants, beaded belts, fringed jackets, hats, neckerchiefs, string ties, specially designed boots, with gloves and wallet to match. There were even chaps and spurs for those times when a young wrangler had to break those wooden broncos in the backyard.

And once you got your cowboy or cowgirl costume, you had to round up your horse. The rocking horse was a traditional toy, but the homebound equine found new importance during the Western craze. It also was improved by the use of a steel framework holding the horse on rugged springs. Suddenly, the wooden carved rocking horse was a shiny, smooth plastic molded spring horse. The constant squeak and rattle of a tiny buckaroo holding on for dear life on a mid-sixties Wonder Horse brand bronc is still a vivid memory today. Giddyap!

You still needed one crucial piece of equipment to complete the transformation into

PISTOLS IN THE LATE FORTIES AND EARLY FIFTIES WERE SIMPLE IN CONSTRUCTION AND STYLE, TOYLIKE AND HARMLESS-LOOKING. BUT AS TIME WENT ON AND TELEVISION HEROES FLOURISHED, TOY GUNS BEGAN TO LOOK MORE REALISTIC.

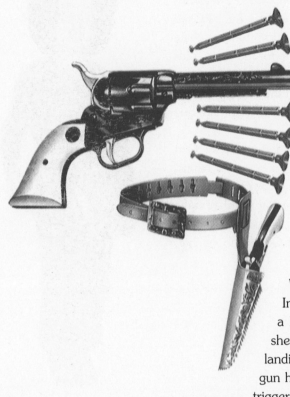

Western hero—a trusty big iron on your hip. You couldn't have a shoot-'em-up without a pistol and a rifle at the ready.

The most memorable was Mattel's Fanner 50. The gun had an enlarged hammer and an especially low-cut holster that enabled you to crouch, draw quickly, and use your other hand to "fan" off a whole set of caps in just a few seconds. It was the weapon of choice for sidewalk showdowns, because you could easily beat your opponents to the draw.

The Winchester saddle gun and accompanying bandolier were also popular Mattel items. Commercials showed Matty Winchester shooting those rampaging Indians with his faithful rifle, dropping in a load of perforated caps, and ejecting shells as he shot away, with most of them landing on the brim of his cavalry hat. The gun held eight bullets, and had a secret trigger mechanism that let you shoot off multiple rounds with one squeeze of the trigger.

The Indian Scout Rifle was a little smaller, but had Shootin' Shell capability, too. The Showdown Set included the Indian Scout Rifle, Buckle Gun, and Fanner with holster, all for just ten dollars. Not surprisingly, Mattel recommended its own Greenie Stik-M-Caps, the round, individual caps designed for Shootin' Shell models, as well as extra Shootin' Shell cartridges and bullet noses at your favorite toy store, too.

Later, Mattel's Crrackfire Winchester replica was guaranteed to sound more authentic than any other rifle. The sound was taken from a Western soundtrack, and the grille over the speaker was designed to look like a cheek rest. Likewise, the Hubley Ric-O-Shay

THE FAST DRAW TIMER TARGET SET GAVE YOUNG SHARPSHOOTERS A THIRTY-TWO-INCH-TALL OUTLAW WITH A TIMER ON HIS CHEST TO TEST THE QUICKNESS OF YOUR DRAW.

gave off a ricochet noise every time it fired, which guaranteed that it would keep those cattle rustlers out of the basement and drive your parents crazy.

The Tru-Blu Handgun, made by the W. J. Murphy Co. ("America's largest manufacturer of Indian dolls") in the fifties was "blued" so that it looked more like the real thing. It was equipped with a real wood grip that you could notch yourself, and was even packaged with a pocket knife for the ritual. Kids were urged to join a nationwide Notch-it Club. There were thirty different sets of Tru-Blu's to choose from. Nichols Industries made the Pinto, a realistic derringer that had a flip-out cylinder and a "pearlescent" grip and would fire one cap cartridge at a time.

Some guns' appeal had nothing to do with realism. Mattel's Buckle Gun featured a belt buckle with a derringer that activated without using your hands. Rather, you surprised outlaws by pushing your belly out, something you could do even with your hands up. The pressure activated a mechanism that made the derringer pop out and fire a Shootin' Shell. If you were caught without your gun behind the corral, there was always the Roy Rogers Quick-Shooter hat.

## THE BIG BANG THEORY

When you took the hat off, you aimed it at your oppressor, smiled, pressed a secret button, and out popped a replica of a derringer that actually fired caps.

Daisy Manufacturing created a "spittin' image" series of guns. One was a model of the "lever-matic" Winchester rifle used on "Lawman," a Western starring John Russell as Marshal Dan Troop and Peter Brown as his young deputy Johnny McKay. At the beginning of the show, as the macho announcer gave their names, Russell tossed the rifle over to Brown. Now you had the opportunity to do the same with your best friend.

The Plymouth Iron Windmill Co., based in Plymouth, Michigan, began in 1882 by manufacturing windmills, but it soon decided that wind power wasn't the wave of the future. When a competitor began selling toy rifles that fired BB shot, Plymouth copied the idea. The company started giving away one of its own BB guns to every windmill buyer. It didn't take long for demand for the guns to outstrip the windmills, and by 1895 the name had been changed to the Daisy Manufacturing Company.

No more windmills.

In 1939 the company signed a contract with cowboy artist Fred Harman to use his popular comic strip character Red Ryder for the name of a new rifle. It was the company's first attempt to create a Western rifle, and it was wildly successful, as millions of kids pretended to be either the old Red Ryder himself, the carrot-topped "famous fighting cowboy," who settled the hash of many an Old West scoundrel, or Little Beaver, the orphaned Indian boy who accompanied him on his adventures across the Southwest. Within a few years, the rifle was sought after by millions of boys.

In 1953 came the introduction of the Daisy toy that would set records: the No. 960 Noisemaker—the BB gun that didn't shoot anything. It looked like a BB gun, felt like a BB gun, worked like a BB gun, sounded like a BB gun, but it

73

shot zip, which made it ideal for those not old enough to have the chance to "shoot their eye out." The S. S. Kresge Co.—the stores with the green front—retailed the Noise-maker for $1.95, and future BB gunners made it the best-selling toy of that year. In 1954, Daisy entered the toy gun-and-holster business.

Other ideas weren't as successful. In 1963 the company contracted with a Japanese firm to make a line of Daisy-matics—battery-operated trucks, fire engines, etc.—but withdrew them a year later when they proved not to be cost-efficient and suggested that the company should "stick to its guns."

To go along with all these toy weapons were miniature Western sets, which included towns, wagons, canoes, horses, stagecoaches, forts, Indians, tents, cacti, trees, ranch houses, tepees, lean-tos, bows, arrows, good guys, bad guys, and anything else you needed to create your own Western ambience. A miniature Wyatt Earp patrolled a metallic Dodge City, with storefront post office, barbershop, Wells Fargo station, bank, and Silver Dollar music hall, which had swinging doors. There were rip-roaring cowboys, fierce Indians, and dastardly robbers to keep little Wyatt busy.

The hundred-piece Alamo set, based on Disney's Davy Crockett trilogy, included Davy and thirty other stalwarts holding out against the forces (thirty plastic toy soldiers strong) of the wicked Santa Ana. With this play-at-home scenario, though, you could change the outcome.

Larger figures were popular, too. American Character's Bonanza Action Men—Ben, Little Joe, and Hoss Cartwright reproduced in stony-faced plastic miniature— could move their heads, hands, and legs and stand, sit, kneel, and ride horseback just like their TV counterparts. For extra play value (not to mention profits for American Character), parents could round up a plethora of accessories for the figures, including a Four-In-One Chuckwagon (Hop Sing, the

FUTURE DICK TRACYS AND SAM CATCHEMS, THE POPULAR COMIC-STRIP SUPERCOPS, COULD PRACTICE WITH AMERICAN CHARACTER'S SILENT RAY-GUN AND TARGET. AN ELECTRONIC MARVEL, IT FEATURED A GUN THAT "SHOT RIGHT THROUGH GLASS" (NO FANCY LASERS HERE; JUST A SIMPLE FLASHLIGHT BEAM).

THESE 1960 GUNS WOULD FIT
RIGHT IN WITH A S.W.A.T. TEAM'S
ARSENAL TODAY.

family cook, was mysteriously absent), to make the imagination run wild if you weren't satisfied with just the Cartwrights themselves.

By the time the Western era ended, other shoot-'em-up TV scenarios had taken their place for a generation glued to the tube: war programs, spy shows, and the perennial standby, the police/detective series.

And to go with these other fantasies, toy manufacturers were busy stamping out guns not just for junior buckaroos. Tommy burp guns (advertised on the Mickey Mouse Club television program, and a replica of the guns used by the Foreign Legion) were popular. One touch of the trigger and the fat gun would send out a stream of shots with a noisy roar while the barrel smoked. And the "sparkling" electric submachine gun fired up to 840 shots a minute with tiny sparks of fire to make it more realistic. Young mercenaries-to-be could practice with a twelve-bullet Browning-type machine gun that swiveled on its tripod base like the real thing. Ack-ack-ack.

If you didn't want to be a cowboy, you could be a detective. Fifties and early sixties television private eyes and policemen were still mostly based on the classic hard-boiled detective novels of the forties. "Martin Kane, Private Eye" was one of the first cops-and-robbers programs on television, debuting in 1949. Played by five different actors in five years, Kane was the epitome of the honorable, intrepid gumshoe.

Kane was soon followed by Rocky King, Ellery Queen, and "The Naked City," the program in which the announcer intoned at the top of the show, "There are eight million stories in the naked city."

Perhaps the most enduring and memorable of all TV cop series was "Dragnet." Jack Webb's Joe ("Just the facts, ma'am") Friday was as impassive as he was moralistic while catching Los Angeles–area criminals in the neverending battle for truth and justice in a world that made no sense. Unlike other cop shows of the day, which were comedic, "Dragnet" was scarily realistic. Conceived and

directed by Webb in a pseudo-documentary style, each broadcast's storyline was culled from actual LAPD criminal files, except that "all the names have been changed to protect the innocent."

Not all crimebusters were so hard-bitten. John Cassavetes' "Johnny Staccato" had problems with his job as private eye. Craig Stevens in "Peter Gunn" got the crap kicked out of him more times than he deserved. "77 Sunset Strip" was, like "Maverick" to Westerns, a spoof on detective shows, with a hip car attendant named Kookie and clever pop-culture references. Both had their own board games. But most followed the formula. "The Untouchables" starred Robert Stack as the lily-white, incorruptible Eliot Ness. Its authentic Prohibition-era clothing, cars, and props, and the steely, film-noir look was picked up by toy makers. Broderick Crawford always barked "Ten-four!" into his squad-car radio in "Highway Patrol," turning it into a favorite kids' catch-phrase.

Soldiers also trooped alongside cops and robbers on TV during the fifties and sixties. Wartime on TV wasn't as popular as Westerns—maybe it was still too soon after the pain and loss of World War II, and the embarrassment of the "Korean conflict" debacle. And war programs nose-dived in popularity by the end of the sixties, when Americans had had enough of Vietnam. But they had a strong impact nevertheless, inspiring boys to pick up authentic-looking carbines and tommy guns and go hunting for enemy patrols in the nearby woods.

War dramas never proliferated like Westerns did, but the pioneering war series of the sixties, such as "Combat" ('62–'67), "The Gallant Men" ('62–'63), "Twelve O'Clock High" ('64–'67), "Convoy" ('65), "Rat Patrol" ('66–'68), set the tone for the make-believe backyard battlegrounds and beachheads defended by the second wave of postwar boys.

MATTEL FOUND ITSELF EQUIPPING AN ARMY OF EIGHT-YEAR-OLD BOYS WITH TOY VERSIONS OF THE LATEST GI JUNGLE CAMOUFLAGE GEAR BEING USED IN VIETNAM. THE M-16 MARAUDER SEMIAUTOMATIC RIFLES WERE JUST LIKE THE ONES THEIR OLDER BROTHERS WERE CARRYING IN THE RICE PADDIES.

TOPPER'S JOHNNY SEVEN O.M.A. ONE MAN ARMY GUN WAS THE PINNACLE OF PRO-WAR HEDONISM. IT COULD LAUNCH A GRENADE, AN ANTI-TANK ROCKET, AN ARMOR-PIERCING SHELL, AND AN ANTI-BUNKER MISSILE, ALL FROM DIFFERENT PARTS OF THE GUN. IT WAS ALSO AN AUTOMATIC REPEATING RIFLE WITH REAL PLASTIC SHELLS, A TOMMY GUN WITH REALISTIC SOUND, AND AN AUTOMATIC CAP-FIRING PISTOL THAT DETACHED AND COULD BE USED SEPARATELY.

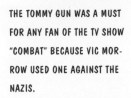

### THE BIG BANG THEORY

"Combat," the best remembered of all the war shows, featured a host of unforgettable roles. Vic Morrow was the brash, emotional Sgt. Chip Saunders, whose signature weapon was a tommy gun, a small machine gun that shot a whole round of bullets in seconds when its lever was pulled back. Rick Jason played Lt. Gil Hanley, the beatific, level-headed leader of the platoon. Pierre Jalbert portrayed Caddy "Caje" Cadron, a Cajun soldier recruited from the swamps of Louisiana; these and the other regulars on the program were easy to identify with. A group of boys could play "Combat" and each kid be assigned to be a corresponding character from the show.

Toy companies caught on to this identification, and created guns, rifles, machine guns, camouflage outfits, plastic helmets, ammo belts, canteens and mess kits, grenades, and walkie-talkies, all in drab olive green. You could buy any number of anonymously manufactured GI-regulation pistols, rifles, and tommy guns. Companies packaged sets such as Halco's U.S. Combat Patrol, clearly based on the TV show, which included a tommy gun, pistol, hand grenade, holster, canteen, and a belt to hang them all from.

By the late sixties, when the oldest baby boomers were in college and protesting against the real war in Vietnam, young kids were playing with updated war gear.

There were plenty of toy versions of tanks, missiles, rockets, planes, helicopters, and every other kind of equipment necessary to wage war. Remco created a huge, battery-operated remote-control tank that lumbered threateningly through many a living room war zone in the late fifties and early sixties.

And as with toy cowboy-and-Indian figures, miniature soldier figures had been the closest boys ever got to playing with dolls. Thanks to the mass-production capabilities of injection-molded plastic, entire armies of green soldiers (or gray and black knights, or red and blue Revolutionary War figures, for the historically minded young general) were available in stores or through comic-book mail order.

THE TOMMY GUN WAS A MUST FOR ANY FAN OF THE TV SHOW "COMBAT" BECAUSE VIC MORROW USED ONE AGAINST THE NAZIS.

TOY ADS WERE OFTEN PLACED IN COMIC BOOKS. AMONG THE MOST UBIQUITOUS ADS WERE MAIL-ORDER FORMS FOR MINIATURE PLASTIC SOLDIER SETS. THE 100-PIECE TOY SOLDIER SET MUST HAVE BEEN TINY, SINCE ALL THE TANKS, BATTLESHIPS, JEEPS, SOLDIERS, WAVES, AND WACS FIT INTO A 6½-INCH-LONG "PASTEBOARD" BOX. YOU COULD ALSO ORDER A CIVIL WAR SET OF 150 SOLDIERS AND THEIR EQUIPMENT (INCLUDING THREE *MERRIMACK* AND THREE *MONITOR* SHIPS).

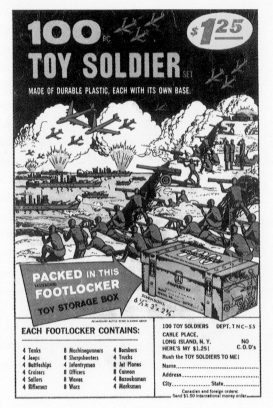

Before plastic made them so inexpensive and easy-to-find, companies produced toy soldier figures from die-cast metal, and often hand-painted them for the most detail. Peco's, an early manufacturer using plastic (they called it Vinylite), applied pre-plastic-age detailing to its relatively large 4½-inch toy soldiers, claiming "The only Really New development in toy figures since 1776." The soldiers grimaced with the effort of doing battle, and their equipment, such as helmets and guns, was detachable.

TROOPS AND ARMORED GEAR INCLUDING MACHINE GUN JEEPS, TANKS, AND ROCKET LAUNCHERS COULD BE TRANSPORTED FROM ROOM TO ROOM OR YARD TO YARD IN A GIANT CARGO PLANE THAT FLOATED IN CASE OF BATHTUB LANDINGS.

The culmination of setting up make-believe battles with toy soldiers was the introduction, in 1964, of G.I. Joe.

The 11½-inch soldier was the first "doll" ever created for boys to play with. The buyers scoffed when G.I. Joe debuted, but first-year sales for the doll topped $16.9 million.

G.I. Joe was a mainstay of the Hasbro company during the sixties. The company was started in 1923 in Providence, Rhode Island, by Henry and Hillel Hassenfeld, brothers who'd immigrated from Poland. Originally named Hassenfeld Brothers, the company sold textile remnants and, later, fabric-covered pencil boxes. In the postwar years, though, the company added toys to its line. In the fifties, it came to prominence in the toy field with its doctor and nurse kits, Mr. Potato Head (which originally consisted of face and body parts you stick into potatoes; the plastic potato wasn't part of the package until later), and Sno-Cone makers shaped like a cheerful Frosty the Snowman.

G.I. Joe pushed Hasbro to the top of the toy market. The idea came out of a TV program whose producers approached Hasbro for a licensing agreement. Don Levine, G.I. Joe's creator, said in 1988 that the secret to marketing a "doll" for boys was never to call it a doll. "It's a movable soldier," he said.

"The Lieutenant" went on the air in September of 1963 and dropped out of sight the next year. Levine kept the idea of a soldier doll in mind, though, and one day happened to see an art-store display of multiple-jointed wooden anatomy models. He bought a dozen and dressed them in scaled-down uniforms as prototypes. For Joe's original face, Hasbro's designers reportedly created a composite of twenty Medal of Honor recipients. The crowning touch was a battle scar Joe wore proudly on his right cheek.

## THE BIG BANG THEORY

He needed a name, though. When the first dolls came off the assembly line with their twenty-one moving parts, they had no suitable identity. Hasbro had agreed to create a doll in all four branches of the military (Army, Navy, Marines, and Air Force), so it had to be a generic fighting name. One night Levine saw *The Story of G.I. Joe,* a 1945 movie about war correspondent Ernie Pyle, and the problem was solved. "GI," a popular term for foot soldiers during World War II, stood for "Government Issue," and reflected the faceless-ness of most soldiers, who were not much more than a number on a dog tag to the government sending them off to war.

The name had been used before Hasbro came upon it, for a 1947 toy called G.I. Joe and His Jouncing Jeep, which was sold with the slo-gan "It speeds, whirls and bucks, but it can't throw Joe!" Hasbro wasn't lax about licensing its best-selling trademark. In 1964, the company announced to the industry that it had registered the name, and "Nobody … but nobody can use the name G.I. Joe except … Hasbro."

Along with its name, G.I. Joe was blessed with its simplicity of concept. Like Mattel's Barbie, who turned five the year Joe was unveiled, the soldier doll was the center of a universe of accessories boys could buy to enhance their fighting fantasies. Joe came with familiar Army wear and gear, right down to clunky black boots, dog tags, and the correct weapons. Hasbro steadily expanded the G.I. Joe line, adding a jeep and a black G.I. Joe in 1965. In 1966, the company introduced the Sol-diers of the World line, which re-created accurate models of Japanese, German, and Russian soldiers, a French Resis-tance Fighter, British Commando, and Aus-tralian Jungle Fighter—now, kids could really set up a prop-er one-on-one hand fight. The company also gave Joe the necessary security clearance to work with the space program, with a Space Capsule set that included equipment to rescue the capsule after a splashdown.

Joe learned to speak in 1967, with a pull-string device that barked out commands such as "We *must* get there before dark … follow me!" Also the same year, Hasbro tried to get sensitive with a G.I. Joe nurse outfit. The doll flopped, and it's since become the most valuable G.I. Joe issue of them all for collectors. Hasbro mounted the first-ever promotional sweepstakes in the toy industry in '67, and created life-sized war toys for boys to

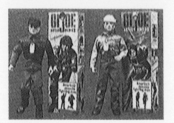

SINCE ITS INTRODUCTION IN 1964, THE MOST FAMOUS MILI-TARY TOY HAS BEEN G.I. JOE.

make believe they were G.I. Joes somewhere behind the lines in the European front.

When it became clear that G.I. Joe's involvement in the Vietnam War wasn't being well received on the home front—Joe had been commissioned as a Green Beret in '66—Hasbro adjusted the soldier's image away from the war. G.I. Joe became part of an Adventure Team, and he and his cohorts went globe hopping in search of adventures that weren't necessarily military in nature. During the early-seventies martial arts craze, the ever-adaptable Joe learned karate, with a special arm mechanism that swung down with a vicious chop at the push of a button. He later even obliged his company's marketing team to become Atomicman, a bionic version of G.I. Joe inspired by the hit TV series "The Six Million Dollar Man."

Alas, Hasbro's efforts to update Joe didn't help sales. In 1978, claiming the high cost of petroleum products because of the worldwide "oil shortage," the company retired G.I. Joe to the same fading mists of memory that General Douglas MacArthur had spoken about during the fifties. There's a happy ending to Joe's story, though. In 1982, Hasbro resurrected him, albeit with a severe height adjustment from a foot tall to four inches, as A Real American Hero, part of a whole new universe of gadgets and accessories. The following year, the new Joe was one of the two best-selling toys of 1983.

G.I. Joe may have taken the country by storm all over again, but he lost one fierce battle. Despite Hasbro's insistence, the United States Court of Appeals for the District of Columbia ruled in 1989 that Joe was a doll. The company had argued that Joe—by then, being manufactured in plants in Hong Kong—was a toy soldier and not subject to higher government tariffs on dolls.

One of the other reasons that wartime toys lost their bang with consumers was that the biggest media escape from the increasingly grim news of Vietnam was in the cloak-and-dagger underworld of spies. By the early sixties, the Cold War had created a cultural dynamic that split the world into the "free" (us) and the "Reds" (them).

Western allies were good guys, and the Russians and other Communists were evil schemers. And with technology advancing the ability of all parties concerned to obtain and analyze top-level communications, the mysterious world of espionage developed an irresistible allure. After American pilot Gary Powers's U-2 reconnaissance jet was shot down over the Soviet Union in 1960 and the Cuban missile crisis two years later, it was obvious that both sides were spying on each other—that this was the way governments worked in the atomic age.

The early pop focus of the spy craze was Ian Fleming's series of novels about the urbane British intelligence officer James Bond, better known to government officials as Agent 007. Though the novels were popular, Bond didn't become the best-known hero of the sixties until the stories were set to script and produced as a series of hit movies (the movies still continue, though Fleming's books have long since been exhausted), originally starring Scottish actor Sean Connery as the suave, clever, womanizing Bond, ace agent of Her Majesty's Secret Service.

*Dr. No* started the gold rush in 1963, followed in quick succession the same year by *From Russia, With Love; Goldfinger* in 1964; and *Thunderball* in '65. That year, 007 sparked a worldwide craze for spy-related paraphernalia, with Bond merchandising keyed into the release.

The character's popularity eventually resulted in a slew of classic TV shows of the mid- and late sixties. Part of 007's appeal was with the arsenal of strange and wonderful gadgets that helped him get out of any jam. The wizard of weaponry that gave Bond all these cleverly disguised gimmicks was Q, the Weapons and Security expert for HMSS. For Bond, he created an Aston-Martin car that shot oil slicks, and had a rotating license plate, bulletproof shield, and a device that came out of its tires to slash away at pursuers. Q had lighters that were really bombs. He had guns hidden in unexpected places. He had all these things that could be reproduced by toy manufacturers for kids to "play" spies.

The Bond movies were often racy, because the Bond character was. How could you not be with female love interests named "Amazon Honeychile" (*Dr. No*), "Pussy Galore" (*Goldfinger*), and "Domino Vitali" (*Thunderball*)? Though toy companies busily cranked out Bond-related ephemera, the biggest

profits would clearly roll in when the Bond formula could be translated into the more family-oriented television medium, to a program that kids could identify with week after week.

So it was no surprise that the first of the spy shows to hit the TV screen was also the one that was most often merchandised by toy companies. "The Man from U.N.C.L.E." was partly conceived with the help of Bond's creator, Ian Fleming. He's the one who came up with the name of the program's lead character, Napoleon Solo, during an early meeting with "U.N.C.L.E." 's producers.

"U.N.C.L.E." stood for "United Network Command for

Law and Enforcement," a fictional worldwide organization that fought despots and evil would-be rulers with the most up-to-date espionage and law enforcement techniques, not to mention the coolest spies since James Bond himself. U.N.C.L.E.'s archnemesis was another worldwide organization, THRUSH, which stood for "Technological Hierarchy for the Removal of Undesirables and the Subjugation of Humanity." That's exactly what U.N.C.L.E. was out to stop.

By 1966, spy-related toys, both licensed and generic, were rampant. Every major manufacturer, including Ideal, Marx, and A. C. Gilbert, as well as dozens of small companies, signed agreements to produce official Bond and U.N.C.L.E. toys. With both fads, guns were the most popular kinds of toys—guns of all kinds, disguised in ever more ingenious ways.

James Bond used Luger guns tucked in a shoulder holster; the U.N.C.L.E. agents used sleeker Beretta pistols with attached silencers, also tucked inside shoulder holsters—all good secret agents had shoulder holsters. That was just the basic weapon.

## THE BIG BANG THEORY

MAJOR MANUFACTURERS GOT ON THE BANDWAGON WHEN THE "MAN FROM U.N.C.L.E." CRAZE ARRIVED, INCLUDING MILTON BRADLEY WITH A CARD GAME AND IDEAL WITH A BOARD GAME.

WHEN "THE MAN FROM U.N.C.L.E." WENT ON THE AIR, THE SUPPORTING CHARACTER OF ILLYA KURYAKIN, PLAYED BY DAVID MC CALLUM, BECAME A SEX SYMBOL. GILBERT RE-CREATED HIS NORDIC GOOD LOOKS IN A GUN-TOTING DOLL.

SPY GADGETS COULD BE SNEAKY AND LUDICROUS AT THE SAME TIME; IDEAL'S U.N.C.L.E. LIGHTER–CIGARETTE CASE–RADIO–GUN WAS A MARVEL OF OVERDESIGN. IT OPENED FROM AN INNOCUOUS-LOOKING LIGHTER INTO AN INSTRUMENT OF DEATH.

American Character marketed lower-end gadgets like the 007 Secret Agent Pen, a regular ballpoint pen on the surface, but actually a deadly useful device for spies. It had a built-in whistle so that "in an emergency, the 007 Pen's high whistle will summon help from fellow agents in school." The pen also shot off caps, and had a switch that sent secret messages hurtling through the air (at least a few feet). The messages were written on the accompanying 007 Vaper-Paper, which dissolved when you dropped it in water. Other accessories from American Character included a secret ring of allegiance, and an ID bracelet with a secret compartment for those pesky secret messages.

For "The Man from U.N.C.L.E.," however, the industry's creative departments went into maximum overdrive. There were dozens of products, from board and card games (Milton Bradley got in the fray with spy-related games, but so did other manufacturers that weren't known for their games), to spy magic kits (A. C. Gilbert sold magic sets emblazoned with 007 as well as U.N.C.L.E., just to cover all bases—never mind that magic tricks had little to do with the spy fad at all), shooting arcades, ordinary walkie-talkies boxed in spy regalia, cars created to match familiar vehicles from the U.N.C.L.E. series (AMT made a beautiful plastic model of the futuristic Piranha car that graced some of the U.N.C.L.E. adventures) and Bond movies, puzzles, bubblegum cards, Halloween costumes, clothes, lunch boxes, books, records…you name it. Ingenious designers even created boxes for U.N.C.L.E. miniature cars that folded out into advertising displays for retail stores.

Several companies also created miniature versions of the famous agents for kids to set up in make-believe situations. Gilbert sold licensed G.I. Joe–like figures for Bond and U.N.C.L.E. characters, as well as a doll for another, short-lived TV thriller series, "Honey West" (starring Anne Francis as a fetching, Bond-like detective). Aurora Plastics offered scale plastic models of Napoleon Solo and Illya Kuryakin, but unless you were a skilled model maker, you were certain to flub the paint job and screw up trying to make the faces realistic.

The biggest boom triggered by the U.N.C.L.E. series (including "The Girl from U.N.C.L.E.," a campier offshoot starring a young Stephanie Powers as April Dancer, which aired in 1966 and '67), though, was in guns. For several years in the late sixties, you could find some of the most cleverly designed toy guns imaginable. Roy Rogers' cowboy hat derringer was a novel idea in the fifties, but it was nothing compared to the plethora of top-secret, hidden, disguised, and just plain strange firearms toy companies later cranked out.

Most guns came with an U.N.C.L.E. logo that gave them the necessary cachet; it was even better if the manufacturer could also include one of the triangular badges that identified U.N.C.L.E. agents on the series. Ideal had a lock on the most popular gun sets, which came with the badge, an ID card, and a cap-blasting Beretta that converted into a rifle with its attachable scope, stock, and silencer barrel. The company also made replicas of the awe-inspiring rifle used by the bad guys in the show, THRUSH agents. The rifle's most prominent feature was the huge red circular night-scope on top of the barrel, and Ideal reproduced the menacing look of the weapon in perfect plastic detail, down to target silhouettes in the sight.

The greatest work of U.N.C.L.E. merchandising, though, was Marx's Counterspy Outfit Trench Coat. The tan vinyl coat was styled to look like the grown-up Burberrys real secret agents wore, but the toy version was designed with a number of secret pockets carrying helpful gadgets from exploding cap grenades to communicators and a couple of guns. The problem was, it didn't take long before the vinyl started to rip. Mom could patch it with clear tape for a while, but within months, you had to trash the coat. By then you'd lost or broken most of the fancy gadgets that came with it, anyway.

The boom in spy toys reached far beyond licensed products keyed in to specific movies or TV shows. Hundreds of generic spy items crowded the toy

ELDON CREATED PHONY CAMERAS, KNIVES, AND PENS THAT WERE ALL TRICK SQUIRT GUNS, THE BETTER TO CATCH ENEMY AGENTS OFF GUARD.

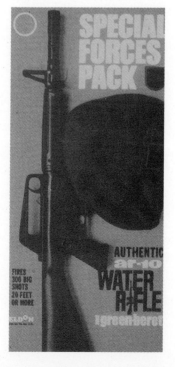

stores and Christmas catalogs of the era, including Mattel's novel Agent Zero M Movie-Shot, a pistol-grip-style movie camera that converted into a deadly machine gun at the press of a button, which activated a telescoping barrel that shot out of the lens.

The relatively new Topper company created its own non-licensed spy gadgets as well: They came with names like Secret Sam, Crime Buster, and Multi-Pistol 09. Though not quite as aggressively violent as the amazing Johnny Seven One Man Army guns, these were pretty handy in fighting the forces of evil espionage.

The Crime Buster was the most macho, a massive machine gun for the kinds of raids that ended your mission. It made a loud siren noise, could shoot bullets, a smoke grenade, or a signal missile. Best of all, it sported a Riot-Spray Gun feature that shot four bullets at once.

Secret Sam was an elaborate heavy-duty pistol-that-converts-to-a-rifle weapon that had a silencer which actually deadened the sound, and could shoot a message missile if you were stuck in distress. You could even attach a periscope to its sight, to aim at the bad guys and still remain hidden. The best part of Secret Sam was the attaché case it came in, which was obviously based on similar cases for 007 and U.N.C.L.E. fans. The pistol fired while it was still in the case, and a real (albeit cheap) camera was built into the case.

With these innovations in fantasy weaponry, it's a wonder that old-fashioned Western guns and holsters are still made. In fact, a quick tour of any toy store will show that young cowboys and Indians still fight it out in backyards all over the country, and a few boys still like to don khaki and olive drab to play army with toy military gear. But you won't find much in the way of spy toys anymore: such is the ebb and flow of cultural fads.

# Going Places

**A**mericans have always been going places—even with their toys. The preferred method of transport has changed over the years from earthbound trains to cars, then skyward to planes and spaceships, but one thing's been constant: the country's restless obsession with motion—forward motion.

The obsession's most manic manifestation in the immediate postwar years was the popularity of model trains and all the paraphernalia that came with them. The popularity of toy trains has long since moved on down the track along with the demise of the real ones, but the spirit's still there if you know where to look for it. Collecting model trains, an avocation with humble beginnings, grew into a cottage industry in the eighties. One magazine devoted to the subject, *Model Railroader,* has a monthly circulation of 200,000, with a newer publication specifically aimed at antique trains, *Classic Toy Trains.*

## THE TOY BOOK

Baby boomers still wax ecstatic about their first train sets, and are spending small fortunes buying back what they probably gave away at a garage sale twenty years ago. And why not? A train set was the encapsulation of a boy's dream. Opening the boxes, with their detailed instruction sheets and layout plans, was incredible enough. But sitting with your setup, a jar of smoke pellets and lubrication kit at your side, the transformer warm in your hands as you moved the engines and cars around the room, you were master of your own universe.

You didn't even need all the fancy stuff. Turn out the lights in the room, and presto, the soft glow from the gleaming Pullman cars, the dispatcher's silhouette in the station, and the bubbling of "oil" from the Sunoco sign on the derrick put you squarely in the mythical town of Lionelville. It's a nostalgic trip into our collective past; in 1950, electric trains were the most wanted toys in America by boys.

Today when nearly everyone flies, and travel by passenger train has almost become an anachronism, it's difficult to grasp how important trains were earlier in the century. The shiny rails of steel were the main source of transportation of material around the country and a staple for long-distance traveling, a chugging, smoking symbol of America's industrial prowess.

MODEL RAILROADING BROUGHT OUT THE BOY IN EVERY GENERATION.

Toy trains had been popular long before the twentieth century. Elaborately designed iron and tin train cars were pulled around Victorian homes. A Connecticut company introduced a windup motor for its tin trains in 1856, which allowed the coupled cars to move in a straight or curved line. By the 1870s, steam-powered engines were introduced, which moved on tracks and were more realistic-looking.

In 1835 a New York blacksmith attempted to show that electricity, then a little understood force, could run a railroad. He was less than convincing, and it would be 1887 before the first electric trolley would be put into service in the United States. By the late 1890s, electric trains were being offered, and by 1901 the Ives Company was selling a windup toy train with track, the same year Joshua Cowen, who earlier had developed the first dry cell battery, began putting electric motors in model railroad cars and selling them as Lionel trains.

Toy electric trains improved year by year and gained in popularity, but the great period of electric trains in America was right after World War II.

The three biggest companies—Lionel, American Flyer, owned by the A. C. Gilbert Co., and Marx—went for the middle-class market. Lionel was the biggest, and had already been in business nearly a half century when it reached its zenith in the fifties.

During the Depression, train sales suffered. Except for an extremely popular Mickey Mouse hand car, made in cooperation with Walt Disney, business was off-track, even for Lionel. The company stopped regular production in 1942 and patriotically retooled for the war effort, manufacturing navigation and communication equipment until 1946, when postwar production really got under way. By 1953, its best year, Lionel sales exceeded $32 million, and the company employed more than two thousand people, which made it the largest toy manufacturer in the world.

Trains were marketed to fathers and sons. Locomotives, especially Lionel's, weren't cheap, so it was important to get Pop into the action and buy all the extras that made the train experience that much more memorable—and lucrative for the makers. Creating classy layouts often took more expertise than most kids were willing to put up with. A common theme of model-train advertising was the simple fact that Dad really played with the train set more than his sons.

The postwar trains had a lot of new extras that dazzled a railroad-hungry public. Lionel began using plastic in 1948, also the year it added diesel locomotives alongside its steamers. Couplers were improved and made more real-istic, radio-wave transmitters were used to control individual cars. American Flyer offered an Electric Eye, actually one of Gilbert's science toys, that magically stopped and started trains with a wave of the hand and turned on layout streetlights with the strike of a match. And cars, well, there were boxcars, cabooses, chemical cars, pipe-carrying cars, gondolas, hop-pers, cement cars, tank cars, crane cars, floodlight cars, baggage cars, observa-tion cars, club cars, Pullmans, coaches, and more, just like in the real world.

But the biggest innovation was smoke. Companies had been strug-gling for years to produce the white stuff that gushed from real locomotives. No matter how realistic they looked, toy trains weren't like real steam engines unless they belched smoke.

Both Lionel and American Flyer came out with smoke the same year. Flyer ads said: "See 'em puff smoke, hear 'em choo choo." Though each had a different smoke system—Flyer's came from a liquid in a capsule inserted in the top of the locomotive tender; Lionel's was an ammonium nitrate pill that smoked when heated, although it was changed later—both companies intro-duced smoke for Christmas 1946. Consumers were giddy with delight.

In 1947 the most popular Lionel "working car," the Auto-matic Refrigerated Milk Car, was introduced. Dozens of action cars realistical-ly moved coal, barrels, oil, logs, ice, and cattle around train layouts, and cranes were a popular moving device, loading and unloading cars and material from one place to another.

But the little milkman in overalls who hauled fresh milk cans from that white plastic "reefer" car onto a green platform day in and day out (what about the poor guy's back?) made the refrigerator car the most popular of all. He was smart; if you slipped marbles or thimbles or anything else besides the milk cans

## GOING PLACES

into the car, he wouldn't deliver them and the whole shebang jammed up. Except that he needed a pair of earmuffs and a coat, he was perfect.

And while models of older locomotives were becoming more realistic, new, modern trains were being introduced.

None was more popular than Lionel's Santa Fe twin diesel super speedliner, the big orange-and-silver monster that already had become a symbol of Americans traveling through the desert Southwest to California in those stylish, double-decker Pullman cars. There was no smoke on this one; it was clean and polished and modern in its design.

The detail on the Santa Fe diesel was incredible; the warbonnet paint scheme, miniature windshield wipers, gleaming knuckle couplers, and markings were painstakingly accurate. At ground level you hardly needed an imagination to think it was the real thing. Flyer and Marx made their own Santa Fe diesels, but both fell short of Lionel's smooth contours.

New gizmos dominated the market as companies tried to outdo each other. In 1947, Flyer trumpeted the introduction of Electronic Propulsion, a ten-dollar phrase for direct current motors. That year's catalog used stroboscopic photographs taken at $1/10,000$th of a second to show how it solved the problem of the train moving back and forth after stops. The next year Electronic Propulsion became Directronic Propulsion, although it was advertised as a new feature. It wasn't long before the feature came equipped with Magnetraction, the insertion of magnets into the locomotive driving axles so they could pull more cars and work better on steeper grades.

Another popular item was the cattle car, introduced by Lionel in 1948. By pressing a remote control button and opening a door at one end of the orange car, you could watch the cattle come out of the car and into a corral with adjustable gates. The cattle moved on a vibrating platform, just like the electric sports games where players vibrated along a rattling metal field. The cattle often fell down or were recalcitrant, and little railroaders found that a little Vaseline on the bases helped cows move more easily.

Factory and industrial themes were popular because the cars actually did something—i.e., load or unload, lift or lower—and because you could incorporate them easily into a layout. For instance, logs could be loaded and unloaded in a forest setting and taken over to the sawmill at the river.

American Flyer came up with its own variations. The Railroad Post Office picked off a sack of mail and delivered it onto a moving train as it swept past. Another flatcar allowed an automobile to go down a ramp off the train. Flyer's Animated Station, introduced in 1953, had a vibrating platform so that little people could board and detrain at the station the way Lionel's cows entered

GIRLS WERE INVITED INTO THE WORLD OF TOY TRAINS IN 1957 WHEN LIONEL INTRODUCED ITS PASTEL TRAIN SET IN "FASHION-RIGHT COLORS."

the stockyard. The Talking Station stopped the train, played a tiny record hidden inside that announced "New York, Philadelphia, Chicago, and all points west, American Flyer through train, all aboard," and started the train back up.

In 1955, Gilbert ads boasted of Flyer's new diesel "roar" units: "From a standing start in the station to full throttle on the main line, all the variety of pulsating big-motor sounds are faithfully reproduced." And we can just imagine how excited it made Mom. In 1956, Flyer advertised via Sugar Pops and Sugar Crisp by giving away miniature adventure series comic books in boxes of breakfast food—a serial in a cereal—with stories like *Highball to Mars, The Ghost Express*, and *Battle of the Table-Top,* printed on real pulp paper stock.

Lionel and Marx both had tracks with three rails, which allowed you to interchange the two; Flyer's was more realistic, with only two rails, but it wouldn't accommodate either Marx or Lionel equipment. (After too many couplings and uncouplings, the tracks bent and didn't work at all, no matter what brand.)

But as with the real thing the great age of toy trains soon faded. Even though companies continued to introduce exciting, cleverly designed cars, sales started to slide. Lionel sales dropped by 38 percent from 1953 to 1955; Flyer sales fell by one-third in the same period. Neither recovered, and in 1959 Lionel was sold to a group of investors. In 1966 Lionel Trains bought American Flyer from A. C. Gilbert.

There were many reasons for the decline: 1957 was the first year that more people traveled by air than by train; the financially rewarding first-class U.S. mail concession moved from rails to air. Trains simply didn't hold up in a time when people were more concerned with how quickly you could reach your destination than how you got there.

On a more direct level, changes in the retail marketplace, such as discount stores that sold trains for less than their catalog value, disrupted a family-owned company like Lionel, which had adhered to traditional marketing procedures, and counted on mom-and-pop businesses to repair and service their intricate mechanisms.

"The existence of the suburbs was both a boon and a bane to Lionel. Enshrined in suburbia was that ideal family to which Lionel addressed itself," Ron Hollander writes in *All Aboard,* his excellent history of the Lionel company. "In the suburbs, Dad as pal, Mom as nurse, sis as audience, and son as Lionel engineer reached their apotheoses. The suburbs provided finished basements large enough to house elaborate electric train landscapes. And the show of financial success that the suburbs represented called for nothing less than a

Santa Fe on Christmas morning. But it was the suburbs that nurtured the shopping center and the discount house that stole customers away from the traditional electric train shops."

As a way of trying to expand its eroding sales base, in 1957 Lionel decided to stop excluding girls from the joys of toy model railroading by introducing a Lady Lionel set. It had a pink locomotive, "robin's egg blue" boxcar, "lilac-colored" hopper, "buttercup yellow" boxcar, and "sky blue" caboose. The transformer was finished in ivory and gold. It was a serious lapse of judgment on Lionel's part. The idea backfired—girls (and their fathers, who had to buy them) hated them—and by 1959 they were gone.

Sputnik also beeped its way around the globe in 1957, and Lionel responded with a miniature version of what would become the MX missile, a moving arsenal of death on the rails. American Flyer matched Lionel with its own rocket-launcher train car, which was made in 1957 and '58. Next to the cattle and milk cars were remote-controlled rocket launchers, radioactive canisters, and nuclear reactor heat exchangers.

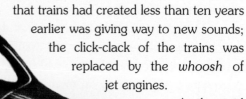

The little flagman and Sam the semaphore man looked as out of place as the quaint, clapboard shacks where they waved at the passing trains. The small-town ambience that trains had created less than ten years earlier was giving way to new sounds; the click-clack of the trains was replaced by the *whoosh* of jet engines.

As the staid Eisenhower era slipped into the past and a young new pres-

94

ident, John Kennedy, looked to the future, model train layouts were replaced by the sleek, fast model slot-car raceways.

It's no secret that Americans have had an ongoing infatuation with the automobile ever since Henry Ford's Model T in 1908. The advent of the Model T's assembly line heralded the modern age of mass production matched by mass consumption.

The allure of the automobile was different from the mechanical fascination with trains—trains were structured; they traveled on schedules along prescribed routes permanently etched with steel guides. But cars represented the most individual freedom ever offered to Americans—they allowed drivers to travel along any damned route they pleased, whether it was the ever-increasing web of four-lane paved roadways crisscrossing the nation (the interstate system was built during the fifties and sixties), the dirt roads wagons had traveled for generations, or even over rough, untamed land. The car wasn't compartmentalized like the train, and it was more civilized, more modern, than riding a horse. It got you farther, which was an important aspect of the automobile's unlimited sense of freedom.

And as cars became more and more commonplace, so did their toy counterparts, which children could push along the floor or ride along the sidewalks and streets, always playing out the fantasy of Going Places. Cars in miniature represented freedom to kids in the same way as real autos did to their parents, even if it was just zooming around the block by foot power.

The only consistent requirement of toy cars was that they be as realistic as possible—the more like Dad's Packard, Hudson, Mustang, or whatever, the better.

Most toy cars were based on full-sized auto designs of the day. And if they weren't miniature replicas of popular models, they managed to evoke a sense of style combining all the major manufacturers' design innovations.

Nosco Plastics of Erie, Pennsylvania, proved you didn't have to stick with automobiles to capitalize on the motoring craze. The company's Motorized Cop-Cycle with "real police siren" was a popular

THE GYRO-WHEEL POWER SYS-
TEM IN KENNER'S SUPER SONIC
POWER CARS MADE THEM THE
BIGGEST-SELLING BOYS' TOYS
OF THE EARLY SEVENTIES.

friction-motor toy. The cycle, complete with uniformed policeman, had an attached sidecar with another cop; the front wheel of the motorcycle adjusted so kids could make it travel straight, or in circles. The cycle, Nosco said, was "a model of motorcycles used by real policemen."

These push-along and windup cars, which appealed to younger boys, had long been part of the industry, with hundreds of anonymous, long-forgotten toys coming and going every year. Few were spectacularly popular, and few managed to create a vivid brand-name association, something toys of the sixties (especially dolls, like Mattel's Barbie) strived for.

One late-sixties Kenner line, the SSP (Super Sonic Power) cars, had plastic chassis ranging from sort-of-realistic autos to souped-up fantasy dragsters. Each car was powered by a large flywheel in the middle of its base. You inserted a ratcheted T-Handle Power Stick into the flywheel and yanked it out, spinning the wheel like a gyroscope.

Kenner capitalized on the popularity of the SSP cars and sold accessories such as a Drag Race Set Unlimited, which came with a timer and a finish line wire that triggered a parachute behind the dragster, and a special carrying case for young collectors. The company also created an SSP Smash-Up Derby, a miniature demolition derby with special cars that flew apart, losing doors, hoods, trunks, and wheels, as they roared off ramps and crashed in midair.

Even toy cars, trucks, and motorcycles needed gas. Scaled-down gas stations and gas pumps have been strategically placed side by side with toy cars on the retail shelves over the years. Amsco, a company not known for its efforts in the toy car market (Amsco's specialty was its line of girls' homemaking toys), made miniature replicas of gas pumps, including a perfectly detailed Magic Gas Pump bearing the Esso (Exxon today) logo. Like the company's popular Magic Cry Baby Bottles, the gas pumps "poured" and "measured" gasoline, then magically refilled themselves in time for the next car to pull up.

One gas station brand didn't bother with gasoline signs—it proudly proclaimed "Marx." Because of its sheer manufacturing volume, Marx was one of the leaders of the toy-car field. Louis Marx had been a director of the successful Ferdinand Strauss toy company, but he broke away to form his own firm in

KENNER INTERNATIONAL SPEEDWAY

1919. He was smart; Marx later bought much of the Strauss line when the older company folded.

Louis Marx & Company built its reputation with mass-produced metal toys that were cheaper versions of popular designs by other manufacturers. The company thrived through support from chain stores and mail-order firms, so in some respects the Marx brand name was one of the best known by American children. By the fifties, Marx was stamping out a mind-boggling array of toys for both boys and girls, including cars and auto-related accessories.

Once you got your own gas station, you set up the hallway as Interstate 35, and put the station at the exit to your bedroom. As the years went by, these self-contained gas stations became more popular than their predecessors on the toy shelves, the elaborate farm sets that came with a menagerie of animals. (About this time, Marx was also busy producing miniature play set pieces that included Western ranch layouts, a complete farmhouse, and even a Robin Hood castle.)

Spurred by the country's burgeoning suburban development and postwar economic boom, manufacturers at the time emphasized heavy-duty gear like tractors, steam shovels, trailers, and trucks—symbols of industry—more than the many kinds of passenger cars. The era of speed and sportiness hadn't arrived yet.

Companies like Structo, Buddy L (which had been manufacturing steel trucks since 1912), Smith-Miller, and Tru-Miniatures were just a few of the better-known brands sending toy cars and trucks off the assembly lines; dozens of other manufacturers also made anonymous toy cars, and the first rash of Japanese tin autos were imported in the late forties. One of the other major brands into the sixties was Eldon, which sold riding toys like a finely detailed locomotive and a fire truck—hoses unreeled, ladders

## GOING PLACES

EVEN DOWN TO THE ADVERTISING
AND THE BRAND NAMES ON SIGNS,
MINIATURE GAS STATIONS LOOKED
LIKE THE REAL THING TO BOYS IN
THE LATE FIFTIES.

extended, and siren worked—in addition to its extensive line of unbreakable Fortiflex plastic pickup and dump trucks, cement mixers, and power shovels.

Tonka Toys, one of the most durable of all toy-auto lines, didn't use plastic because its nearly indestructible line of toy trucks was manufactured by its parent company, Mound Metalcraft Inc. of Mound, Minnesota. The company was started in the basement of an old schoolhouse in 1946; its first products were tie racks and garden tools. The next year, Mound Metalcraft bought out a failed toy company that had unsuccessfully tried to market a steel steam shovel. Mound ironed out all the kinks in the shovel, sold it under the brand name "Tonka Toys" along with a crane, and had a hit on its hands. The toys were named after nearby Lake Minnetonka; the word *tonka* also meant "great" in Sioux.

Between 1949 and 1951, the company branched out and made dolls' beds, and in the mid-sixties it briefly sold barbecue grills, but otherwise, Tonka concentrated on trucks, construction equipment, and heavy-duty cars. In 1949, Mound Metalcraft manufactured thirteen different Tonka vehicles; in 1959, the company, which had changed its name to Tonka Toys in '56, sold forty-three models. The Sanitary Service System Truck, a garbage truck that came with a dumpster, won an award as one of the ten best toys of 1959 from *Science and Mechanics* magazine.

During its heyday, Tonka was a veritable giant among miniature trucking companies. Its line included fleets of semitrailers, an Allied Van Lines moving truck, Green Giant grocery transport truck, Star-Kist Tuna van (the brand-name associations made the trucks that much more realistic), logger truck complete with a load of plastic logs, and a livestock van.

In 1961, Tonka purchased a plastics company and started selling accessories for its cars and trucks. In 1962, Tonka's Surrey Jeep was one of the biggest-selling toys of the year. More than half a million miniature jeeps were sold that year, helping

EVERY KIND OF VEHICLE WAS
REPRODUCED BY TOY CAR MANU-
FACTURERS—EVEN A TRAILWAYS
BUS, WITH A WORKING LUGGAGE
COMPARTMENT AND SPARE TIRE.

boost Tonka's sales to more than $10 million. Other popular models of the sixties included 1964's Mighty Dump and 1966's Volkswagen Bug. The company's still going strong today, with its reputation for quality construction and hard-playing durability intact.

Another company, Topper, got into the toy truck race in 1965 with its sturdy, remote-controlled (by wire—it wasn't a radio control) Johnny Express tractor-trailer rigs, which were designed with interchangeable loads, including a crane, dump truck, troop carrier, pipe hauler, and van. Accessories included a conveyor loader, forklift, and cargo (wooden pallets, crates, and miniature steel drums). The system's claim to fame was that it was reinforced with steel, and could handle the weight of a 200-pound man standing on its truckbed.

For kids—mostly boys, when it came to toy cars—who were older, companies stepped in with more sophisticated cars. The L. M. Cox Manufacturing Company, later Cox Hobbies, is well known for its gas-powered planes, but it also filled a growing (older) market niche with its scale-model automobile replicas, which were powered by Cox's high-performance gas engines.

Cox's production line started up in 1946 with basic "push-pull" racing cars, and first added engine-powered models in 1948. By the late fifties, Cox had added a number of airplanes, many—like the P-40 Flying Tiger and Stuka Dive Bomber—based on famous fighter planes from World War II. The company also introduced model rockets and rocketry kits starting in 1969 and through-

### GOING PLACES

SLOT-CAR SETS BROUGHT FATHERS
AND SONS TOGETHER, THE SAME
WAY TRAIN SETS HAD A DECADE
EARLIER.

out the seventies and into the eighties. The company still runs strong with its motorized models.

Throughout the sixties, Cox created 1:24 scale versions of well-known autos such as Ferrari and Lotus, Ford GT, the 1963 Buick Riviera, and even a model named after famed racer Jim Hall's Chaparral for budding "gear-heads." The Ferrari Dino model, made of injection-molded plastic, was a sterling example of Cox's attention to realism: it featured a detailed interior, complete with a driver. In a 1971 advertisement for its fourteen-inch Baja Bug, Cox proudly outlined its powerful drive. "You can't get this kind of go with power cells or batteries," read the ad. "You need the real thing: a gas engine. The Cox .049 internal combustion engine.

Just like the one in your father's car. Only smaller—about half the size of your hand. And actually more perfectly engineered than the one in his car."

The attraction of gas-powered model cars was that, like the grown-up counterparts, the cars moved under their own power. They felt, even sounded, like real cars instead of immature toys. As symbols of automotive freedom, they were reined in only by the tether you could attach to make them go in circles; otherwise, you could set a car on a quiet suburban street and watch it go straight down the block.

But by the mid-sixties, even the giant of motorized model cars had to take

A NATIONWIDE RACING PROMOTION SPONSORED BY AURORA WAS SO POPULAR THAT IT OFFICIALLY KICKED OFF THE SLOT-CAR CRAZE IN 1962.

notice of the fad that had finally overtaken the model train's lock on the American imagination: Cox introduced slot cars to its line in 1964.

Slot cars were much like trains in several respects. Both took up large amounts of space and needed layouts to be successful. Like trains, slot cars and their accessories were big-ticket items—you could spend as much as your budget would allow. And like the mighty locomotives, they were often *the* thing in most boys' minds on Christmas morning.

Slot cars were similar to model trains in that they were powered by an electric transformer that fed current to the inset slots that ran along every piece of "roadway" track. The similarity was no accident: though motorized toy cars had been around since the thirties, it wasn't until after World War II that a few enthusiasts in England and the United States tried fitting scale-model cars with engines taken out of electric model trains. The first slot cars worked with crude

## GOING PLACES

train-set transformers, which couldn't be controlled except to turn on at full speed or completely off.

When manufacturers caught on to the potential windfall, they came up with more practical designs. The power fed into each slot was individually controlled by a separate hand control for each driver—the more you pressed down on the control plunger with your thumb, the faster your car zipped along the track. The trick was to learn to control the power, so you didn't take a curve too fast and spin out of control, jumping out of the slot and likely off the track altogether, landing unceremoniously on the basement floor.

Each car had a prong underneath that slipped into the groove of the slot, and its metal conductor picked up the electricity to run the motor that drove the track-gripping foam or rubber tires. To make sure the conductors worked smoothly, drivers would tinker with their copper wires, twirling them ever

tighter, then smearing saliva on them to make them "hotter." The last thing you needed was for your car to hesitate when you rammed down the speed control.

The speed, as well as the competitive nature of slot-car racing, caught the imagination of young and old Americans alike in the early sixties. Even as sales of home slot-car sets were booming, public slot-car tracks opened up in storefronts across the country, offering hotshot "drivers" the chance to take on neighborhood champions and even strangers in a pool hall–type environment.

These public tracks had room-filling race courses with multiple lanes, up to eight or twelve cars side by side at the starting line. The contenders would enter the raceways, favorite car in hand, and sign up a slot for the next race. The country was even more obsessed with model motoring than it had been just a decade earlier with model railroading. Setting up the most elaborate train sets in your basement was a private pursuit, but working up adrenaline by beating other racers with skill and a good car was a public and very social activity.

By 1962, *Playthings* magazine reported that the most excitement at the Toy Fair of that year was being generated by the roadway layouts and the new

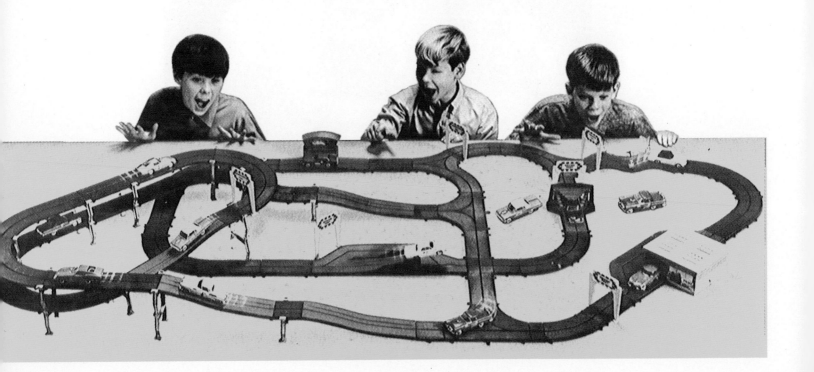

gimmicks of the half-dozen producers of slot cars. By the next year, there were three times as many manufacturers of cars and accessories, and great improvements were made in equipment like lap counters, reversing switches, bridges, fences, scoreboards, and pit service centers.

Aurora Plastics Corp.'s wildly successful Ford Grand National Model Motoring Competition, a nationwide series of races held by retailers and promoted by the manufacturer, brought crowds to toy stores. During the spring and summer of '62, more than a million contestants signed up for a shot at being neighborhood champions, and millions more stood by and were hooked enough to buy their own slot-car sets. Following a PR coup—a story in *Look* magazine that July—the national finals were held in New York City.

Revell, the major plastic-model manufacturer, realized early on that the slot-car craze would go beyond home setups, and was the first to sell components separately, for the "professional" slot-car hobbyist to build his own custom racers. Revell also aggressively created slot-car kits in both 1:32 and 1:24 scale sizes: detailed copies of real-life racing cars such as the '65 Corvette Sting Ray, Ford Cobra, Lotus 23, and Porsche RS-60.

Another parallel between slot-car racing and model railroading was that the track layouts weren't cheap. That's why ads always showed parents having fun, too—they're the ones that had to shell out the hard-earned bucks down at the hobby shop. Revell's 1965 sets started with the "budget-priced" Enduro, which sold for $30. The best-selling Gran Turismo racing set, which came with the 'Vette and a Ferrari GTO 250, retailed for $40. The Europa, a huge figure-eight layout—featuring classy European cars, a Mercedes and an Aston-Martin—came with seven straight and sixteen curved pieces of track, as well as spinout aprons and bridge supports to make the course interesting, all for a measly $55. And Revell's crowning achievement in home layouts, the four-lane Americana, tapped Pop's wallet for $85.

Strombecker's road-race sets were slightly less expensive, but comparable in features. In 1963, Strombecker's most expensive four-lane figure eight retailed for $64.95. One $25 model, the Hiway Patrol Set, was an oval track with two lane-crossing intersections that afforded cars the thrill-a-minute possibility of disastrous crashes—drivers had to be quick with their control knobs to slow down or speed up to avoid collisions. Especially since one of the cars that came with the set wasn't a racer, but a police car, complete with flashing red lights and a siren. The other car? A hot rod—the type any self-respecting juvenile delinquent would drive.

By the late sixties, car racing had become so popular that toy companies were scrambling to find ways to capitalize on the fad, coming up with sets for younger kids.

The Ideal Corp. also got into the model car market with its mid-sixties catalog of Motorific cars, trucks, and tracks. But the company decided to avoid the slot cars' complicated array of required accessories (special tracks, transformers), and made each car run independently, with its own motor, which ran on two penlight batteries. That way, kids could turn on the motor and preset the cars to travel straight or in turning positions on living room floors and down hallways. The Motorific tracks, which were heavily advertised on TV, simply contained a groove for the cars to travel along.

Another smart feature of Ideal's slotless slot cars was that their body chassis all fit on one motorized, battery-operated automotive base. So kids could collect a dozen different bodies and have to maintain only one set of wheels. The company expanded the Motorific line with tough-looking Motorific trucks, which also all fit on one standard six-wheeled base.

Mattel sold a similar concept in non-slot-car race tracks. Its Switch 'N Go autos were individually battery-powered, like Ideal's Motorific. But the bright plastic Fastback GT racers were hooked up to a "track" of plastic tubing and accordionlike Air Switches. The flexible tubing guided the cars in any shape roadway you wanted; the switches controlled such features as a four-way bridge crossing, gates that flipped over cars traveling the wrong way, and intersections where drivers could choose their turns. Mattel's line of car styles, however, wasn't nearly as varied or as realistic as Motorific's.

By the seventies the novelty of slot-car racing and even the less restrictive motorized toy cars had worn off, and manufacturers had to discover new ways to keep the excitement alive. One way was to shrink the cars even more to the tiny HO scale that had been created years earlier to make trains practical for home setups. Tyco Industries' TycoPro HO-scale slot-car line was

BASEBALL GREAT WHITEY FORD PEDDLED MATCHBOX CARS IN PUBLICATIONS FROM *BOYS' LIFE* TO *THE NEW YORK TIMES.* NOTICE THAT FORD'S HOLDING ON TO A MATCHBOX TRACTOR THAT'S OBVIOUSLY DRAWN IN AFTER THE FACT.

heavily promoted in focus-group publications as *Boys' Life,* so every scout in the country knew about them. These days, the few toy and hobby shops that still carry slot cars sell only HO-scale sets. It's an ironic turnaround, considering how model railroading has once again become popular.

Even Ideal retooled its Motorific line, and came up with the HO-sized Mini Motorific series, which used even smaller batteries than penlight-size. Big cars were out; small—hell, tiny—cars were in.

Tiny automobile replicas were nothing new, but a new feature, introduced in 1969, was about to eclipse the slot-car craze of a few years before. The entire toy-car industry was about to shift into high gear again.


The most familiar American toy-auto manufacturers were names like Tootsietoy (a company started in the 1890s, and renamed in the 1920s after a founder's granddaughter's nickname, Toots), Hubley, Dent, Marx: names revered today by collectors. But the best miniature cars—more scale models than toys—started out as imported specialties.

Corgi, a brand name that still has a "top-end" reputation for its finely detailed car miniatures, was established in 1956 by Mettoy Playcraft Ltd., a Welsh manufacturer. The company's emphasis from the start was on realism. Even the first Corgi Toys were advertised with the phrase "The ones with windows," as opposed to a lithographed illustration of a window, or worse, none at all. To do battle in the marketplace with England's best-selling toy cars, which were produced by Dinky (since it no longer exists, Dinky cars are valued collectibles), Corgi went out of its way to add innovative features. From early on, Corgi's autos had movable parts, like doors that opened to reveal detailed interiors, hoods that lifted to reveal a realistic engine block.

By the mid-sixties, Corgi was selling a number of novelty cars as well as replicas of real models. Corgi licensed the rights to manufacture such novelties as a Batmobile, a James Bond Aston-Martin with flip-up bulletproof shield and a plastic driver that ejected out of an emergency seat, and a Man from U.N.C.L.E. car. The four-inch-long U.N.C.L.E. sedan didn't look like anything from the popular mid-sixties TV spy series, but when you pushed down on a rooftop siren, tiny figures (they didn't look much like Napoleon Solo and Illya Kuryakin, either) popped out of their seats and fired pistols as if in hot pursuit of evil THRUSH agents.

With its heavy-duty die-cast construction, detailing, and extra moving parts, Corgi has been a perennial favorite in the miniature toy-car world. In

Great Britain, another company created its niche in the industry with its even smaller-sized autos and novel packaging.

Leslie Smith and Rodney Smith had been schoolfriends in England, and met up again during World War II, when they both served in the Royal Navy. In 1947, with Britain's economy on the road to recovery, the two friends combined their first names and their dreams of owning a business and formed the Lesney Corporation, making die-cast metal industrial parts. In 1949, the company added some small toys as a way of offsetting the off-season. By 1953, the off-season products evolved into a 1:75 scale line of miniaturized cars trademarked under the name of Matchbox, which were appropriately packaged in small cardboard boxes modeled after a matchbox.

The Matchbox concept was a hit in England, where Lesney created palm-sized replicas of everything from tractors and trucks

AS A RESPONSE TO THE IMMEDI-ATE SUCCESS OF MATTEL'S HOT WHEELS, MATCHBOX CREATED ITS SUPERFAST SERIES OF CARS WITH FRICTIONLESS WHEELS AND PLASTIC TRACKS.

### GOING PLACES

STOP AND GO: TOOTSIETOY'S SUPER SERVICE STATION NOT ONLY "FILLED UP" MINIATURE CARS AND TRUCKS, IT FOLDED UP INTO A STORAGE AND CARRYING CASE.

to ambulances, double-decker buses, and every auto brand. In 1954, the company found an American distributor.

The immediately identifiable Matchbox Series boxes became a cornerstone of the toy-auto market, even holding their own during the slot-car years. Mettoy over in Wales took notice, and introduced its Husky line (later renamed Corgi Junior) of smaller-scale cars in 1964, hoping to lure some of Matchbox's fans. One late-sixties Matchbox ad proudly hypes a handy carrying case with enough space for seventy-two cars, and plenty of kids had that many they needed to store.

In 1969, the toy-car industry was caught off guard when Mattel introduced its Hot Wheels miniature cars, which were equipped with frictionless soft wheels that allowed the cars to travel great distances at great speed with just a slight push on smooth yellow plastic tracks.

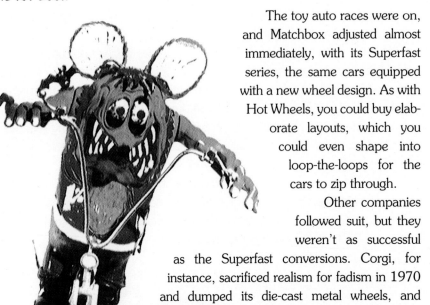

The toy auto races were on, and Matchbox adjusted almost immediately, with its Superfast series, the same cars equipped with a new wheel design. As with Hot Wheels, you could buy elaborate layouts, which you could even shape into loop-the-loops for the cars to zip through.

Other companies followed suit, but they weren't as successful as the Superfast conversions. Corgi, for instance, sacrificed realism for fadism in 1970 and dumped its die-cast metal wheels, and replaced them with low-friction plastic tires called Whizzwheels. Mettoy even came out with a separate Corgi Rockets line that year designed to fit Mattel's Hot Wheels track. Hot Wheels' hold on the market was so strong that the Corgi Rockets series was produced for only two years.

THE APTLY NAMED "FUNNY CARS" MADE FOR EVEN FUNNIER MODELS, WITH MONSTERS AT THE WHEEL.

While toy car fads came and went, one part of the industry remained stable: plastic model kits. During the sixties heyday of modeling, you could enjoy the familiar smell of plastic cement and Testor's enamel paints in every basement family room, where kids (mostly boys) assembled everything from elaborate replicas of ships, airplanes, and cars of every style and color to see-through educational scale models of the human body. The glue

would smear and melt the plastic seams; the paint would run and drip on Mom's avocado carpet (no matter the precautions you took with newspaper to cover it); pieces would somehow always get lost or there would be one or two left over after you finished.

For most budding hobbyists, making models was a messy pain in the butt, but everyone made them, so you did too. Brand names like Revell, Hawk, AMT, ITC (the hobby division of the Ideal Toy Corporation), and Monogram beckoned to customers not just in toy stores but in hobby shops and drugstores (every drugstore seemed to have an aisle devoted to model kits and the endless array of tiny paint bottles in bright solids and wild metal-flaked colors).

Revell was one of the first to enter the model hobby kit market. At the end of World War II, an entrepreneur named Lew Glaser bought a failed plastics company for the meager sum of $700 and launched Precision Specialties with a Minnie Mouse washing machine and a Maxwell auto pull-toy. When he introduced them in 1950, the Maxwells were so popular that Glaser was urged to skip some of the production steps and release the car as a model kit, and let buyers assemble it themselves. Glaser declined at first, but the next year, when demand slipped, he decided to make the Maxwell the first kit produced by his renamed company, Revell Inc. Over the next few years, Glaser's model kits established Revell so strongly that the company turned away from making toys and drove off into the sixties on plastic wheels.

The best car models, such as Revell's, prided themselves on their accurate details and realism—the whole point was to copy exactly a notable auto, and to capture its spirit on a smaller scale. But even the modeling industry succumbed to car fads.

During the early sixties, while California dreaming was being put to song by the Beach Boys and Jan and Dean, and the surfing craze was taking to the streets, the beachcomber life-style begat a bizarre collection of fantasy auto-mobiles driven by the ugliest monsters anybody had ever seen. These twisted hot rods were caricatures of the fun-in-the-sun California life-style, and they sparked a decade's worth of weirder-than-ever designs.

The king of the monster cars was Ed "Big Daddy" Roth, a cartoonist with an eye for hot rods and monsters who first brought his designs to life in 1963 for Revell. Not all of them were garish 3-D cartoons: Roth also created deli-cate, believable dragster and hot rod designs that were typical of the beach scene's devotion to sleek, hip wheels. His futuristic cars had names like the Outlaw, Beatnik Bandit, and Mysterion, and one—the tiny, surfboard-carrying Surfite—was even created for real and used in the 1965 film *Beach Blanket Bingo.*

But Roth's stock-in-trade was the funny monster cars, and his most famil-iar character was Ratfink, a huge rodent behind the wheel of a funny car, with bulging, bloodshot eyes, gaping mouth with pointy teeth, and tongue flapping in the wind. Variations of that character became known as other Finks: Super Fink, Angel Fink, and so on. In 1965, Revell held a contest to name the newest Fink; the winner received a visit from Roth at the neighborhood hobby shop. One of Roth's early creations, Mr. Gasser, was made with "customized eye-balls," and could stand alone without the car. In fact, Roth's designs reduced the importance of the car: the ad for Mr. Gasser mentions, as an afterthought, "'57 Chevy with blown engine included with monster."

It didn't take long for Roth's ideas to be taken to their goony extremes. Suddenly monster cars had names like Shift Kicker and Freaky Rider. The Hawk Model Co. flooded the market with Roth knockoffs in its Weird-Oh line, with names like Davey the Psycho Cyclist, The Digger, Wayout Dragster, and Daddy the Swingin' Suburbanite. Hawk even made a monster jetfighter, Fred-dy Flameout, which promised to "scare you out of ten years' growth and you'll love every minute of it."

Also in the late sixties, Revell signed on another popular fantasy-car illus-trator, Dave Deal, to design some freaky autos of his own. Deal's Wheels included two Volkswagen variants, the Bug Bomb and Glitter Bug. Deal didn't place too much emphasis on the creatures driving his cars; he stuck to warp-ing the appearance of the cars themselves.

As the seventies drew on, and terms like "gas shortage" and "oil spill" entered the American consciousness, wacko funny cars somehow didn't seem as funny. Bigger, faster, louder, and grosser didn't have the same appeal when

## GOING PLACES

AT THE HEIGHT OF SLOT-CAR RAC-
ING'S POPULARITY, COMPANIES
SUCH AS TYCO SOLD SEPARATE,
SPECIALLY DESIGNED (WEIGHTED
TOWARDS THE FRONT WITH A
"TRICK" PIN TO SLIP INTO THE
TRACK SLOT) CARS FOR USE ON
ANY NEIGHBORHOOD TRACK.

practical features like four-wheel drive and gas efficiency were primary concerns at the car dealers.

And as kids grew up and out of needing Dad to help buy elaborate slot-car sets—and into driver's licenses and real cars of their own—model racing slowed down. You'd be hard-pressed to find a public slot-car raceway these days, except in isolated pockets around the country.

Hot Wheels, Corgi, and Matchbox have all survived with their popularity intact (Matchbox was sold in the eighties to a Hong Kong–based die-cast manufacturer). But the big craze these days is for ever more complex radio-controlled cars, which can easily cost more than $100.

# The Ride Stuff

**W**hen Antonio Pasin, an Italian immigrant who'd worked in the Chicago sewers and Minnesota mineshafts, found himself making more and more wooden tool wagons for his co-workers, he decided to go into business. He started the Radio Steel & Mfg. Co. in 1929, just at the start of the Great Depression. His wagons, which he dubbed Radio Flyers, turned out less functional than entertaining, but they were a big hit.

When he started mass-producing his wagons, Pasin constructed them out of steel instead of wood. A shrewd businessman, he bought the steel from automobile manufacturers, who sold him the scrap sheets left when window holes were cut in auto bodies. Those sheets just happened to be the perfect size for Pasin's wagons, which were molded out of one piece, with rounded edges and smooth-rolling wheels.

### THE TOY BOOK

By 1933, Radio Steel & Mfg. had an exhibit at the Chicago World's Fair, with a lavish showroom in the shape of a boy on a Radio Flyer leaning forward into the wind—and presumably, into the future. Just a few years later, when Radio Flyers had become "Young America's Finest Coaster Wagons," Pasin unveiled what may be the greatest wagon ever sold. "Our special holiday number for 1936, the deluxe Streak-O-Lite Model 1000," was streamlined to look like a Depression Moderne car and was equipped with electric headlights, an instrument panel decal modeled after a Packard's dash, an electric horn, and Buick hub caps. Unlike the rest of Radio Flyer's line, which had been an unvarying rich red, the Streak-O-Lite was cream-colored with red accents.

Wartime demands slowed Radio Steel during the early forties, but when the company came out of World War II, Radio Flyers were ready to roll with the new generation. By then, the Radio Flyer name was available on both wagons and scooters. The 1946 catalog promised "full prewar quality" on "the big, strong, handsome" Radio Flyer, the basic model. Two smaller models, the American Beauty and the Radio Special, were also available, but they had just "Flyer" stenciled on their bright red sides. Only the main model sported the curling, speedy-looking "Radio Flyer" logo and semi-inflated rubber tires for the smoothest ride.

By the early sixties, the company had begun to manufacture garden carts and wheelbarrows, and offered twelve different Radio Flyer wagons and four scooters, from tot-sized (the Radio Tot scooter was a three-wheeler) to wagons with removable steel panels to increase capacity for grown-up work. The Radio Town & Country, a stake wagon with a hardwood body and wooden slat sides, was a nod to Antonio Pasin's ingenuity and determination.

Other manufacturers also sold wagons over the years, including

## THE RIDE STUFF

Streater Industry, whose Station Master stake wagon made its debut in 1947; and Happi Time, whose line of wagons was featured in Christmas catalogs throughout the fifties. And many companies sold other types of rideable toys, called velocipedes in the industry.

In the immediate postwar years, most riding toys were modeled after the streamlined, futuristic look of thirties industrial design. Even baby carriages (real ones, not ones for dolls) like the Murray-Go-Round rolled with elegant modernism. The Garland Red Flyer, introduced with great fanfare in 1947, was a riding dump truck with a hydraulic bed that "automatically lowers the tailgate and dumps the load of blocks, sand, marbles or other cargo, just like a big dump truck." The truck, which resembled the front end of a thirties railroad engine, was allegedly designed by " 'big time' engineers in the automotive industry."

Not all riding toys were as easy on the eyes. Some were designed for practicality, not style. The Tru-Matic push shovel from 1947 looked like a gawky Erector set project gone out of control, but its digging scoop could be adjusted, using a hand lever and hand crank, for depth of digging and length of stroke. For a more traditional-looking piece of equipment, kids that same year could opt for a Tru-Matic Combination Bulldozer/Road Roller/Road Scraper. Unlike the riding cars, both these Tru-Matic toys were push-powered, not pedal-powered.

After World War II, the boxy, utilitarian jeep became another symbol of American might and dependability. And it didn't take long for miniature jeeps to start rolling down new suburban sidewalks. The Junior-Pro Jeep was one of the first, introduced in 1947. "It's a real honest-to-goodness child-size Jeep that's built strong and durable like the rugged, multi-purpose Army Vehicle!" an ad boasted. The steel car was painted a bright green and held three kids, presumably all up-and-coming soldiers.

The St. Louis–based Junior-Pro Products Co. had one intriguing feature for its jeep that other companies didn't have: the toy was sensational, the company said, because it was "A Child-Size JEEP that's Equipped for Electric Motor and Battery!" Alas, just like at the grown-up car dealers, there was small print: "Foot pedals are standard equipment."

GARTON UNVEILED ITS VISION FOR THE FUTURE IN 1954. THE THREE-WHEELED SPACE CRUISER WAS A ROCKET-SHAPED GEM FOR EVERY KID ASPIRING TO BE BUCK ROGERS; IT EVEN HAD A SPACE GUN MOUNTED ON ITS SIDE, WHICH SHOT A PROPELLERLIKE SPINNING "DART."

The manufacturers of riding toys turned all kinds of vehicles into small, pedal-driven packages. Sears' or Montgomery Ward's Christmas catalogs featured everything from tiny hook-and-ladder fire engines to police cars, trains, trucks, dragsters, tractors, and farm equipment, as well as unfamiliar designs that weren't based on anything grown-ups had. Some companies outdid themselves in the quest for novel riding toys, however.

During the height of the sixties Batman craze, Marx created a hard-plastic Batmobile which sold for $15.66. The toy wasn't pedal-powered; it contained a noisemaking motor that was wound by backing up the Batmobile a few feet, which surged the car forward as the steel spring unwound. The Batmobile came complete with a Bat-cape made of such flimsy vinyl that it ripped to shreds within a week. In the seventies, Marx's great triumph in the wheel-goods market was the production of the Big Wheel, a low-slung tricycle that combined elements of hot rods and bicycles, and was manufactured almost completely of plastic: plastic seat, handlebars, frame, and even wheels. The Big Wheel became popular with older kids in the early seventies, when high-school students would raid neighborhood yards and steal them away to race down hillsides.

The Irwin Corp., which had been making toys since 1925, came up with some of the best ad copy ever for its 1961 line. The Moto Scooter, based on the popular European Vespa Scooters, was "actually a real bicycle," the company promised. "Remove trainer wheels and you have a real chain driven moto scooter." Another model, the Deluxe Pedal Action Motocycle, also was built to look like a motorcycle. A third model, the Deluxe Racer, was a decent facsimile of an Indy race car. All three Irwin toys had a "strong lightweight one piece body of 'Irvilon 777'"—plastic. Another Irwin ad for its Pedal Rider Motor Cycle also touted its "easy operating pedal drive," "realistic and authentic engine detail," and body made of "steel and steelstrong plastic." It's all in the marketing.

In the end, the basic riding toys—cars, tractors, and wagons—outlasted gimmicky wheel goods. Of course, that didn't mean wagon makers didn't try some silly variations too. Big Boy's Moon Wagon, which came along in the wake of the 1969 lunar landing, was nothing more than a goofy circular wagon with mod flower decals inside and an extra wheel mounted at an angle in the back. The wagon allowed kids to pull bicyclelike "wheelies" and roll along with the front end aimed skyward. The idea was a reworking of one dreamed up by Garton, usually one of the steadiest manufacturers in the field, earlier in the sixties.

All this silliness led to the ultimate riding toy: the bicycle. A child's introduction to cycling began with the tricycle, the sturdy little three-wheeler that didn't need a balancing act to pedal. But the real thing was the two-wheeler. All kids remember the Christmas or birthday when they were given their first bicycle, usually with training wheels so the young rider wouldn't fall over. And no one forgets the feeling of total freedom the first time you rode it without Mom or Dad helping, that moment when you were no longer confined to your legs for self-transportation.

For being a foundation of the wheel goods toy industry, the bicycle has a relatively short history. The first bicycles, created in Europe in the late 1700s, were called "walka-longs," because the riders straddled their cross beams and pushed themselves along by foot. By the mid-1800s, two-wheelers came with pedals on the front wheel for propulsion, but it wasn't until about 1880 that the modern bicycle, with two equal-sized wheels and a chain drive, became popular. In 1889, the air-filled rubber tire was introduced, and bicycling became the rage of the United States—by 1899, 312 American manufacturers were making cycles.

Combining utilitarian virtues (they are, after all, a viable form of transportation) with a sense of fun, bicycles still hadn't changed much by the late forties, except that fewer companies manufactured them. The most memorable brand names of the past few decades are still around today: Murray, Huffy, Schwinn, and Raleigh. Others have faded with time: Evans, Hawthorne, Hercules, and J. C. Higgins, Sears' line. Sears sold its own line of Spyder bikes during the sixties heyday of banana-seat high-rise cycles.

In the postwar years, bicycles often were designed to look like cars, because Americans already were obsessed with automobiles and the best creative industrial design in the country was going into automobile production.

EVANS USED THE SAME DESIGN FEATURES ON BOTH TRICYCLES AND BICYCLES WHEN IT UNVEILED ITS 1960 MODELS.

HUFFY BIKES IN 1969 WERE "LONG, LOW AND LEAN JUST LIKE THE SLEEK RACERS AT THE DRAG STRIPS." THEY CAME WITH GLEAMING, METAL-FLAKE PAINT JOBS AND VINYL BANANA SEATS THAT GLITTERED WITH OUTLANDISH COLORS OR MOD FLOWERS.

## THE RIDE STUFF

The Murray Ohio Manufacturing Company's 1950 line of Mercury Bicycles featured the fat balloon tires of the day, as well as aerodynamic detailing stolen right from the automobiles they were named after. For genteel enthusiasts, the ultimate cycling machine was the English-style touring bicycle, which featured three adjustable gears.

Within a few years, some cycles became less utilitarian in design, and more garish for entertainment's sake. With a ready-made and growing market of children too young for cars, manufacturers began aiming their creations more and more at them.

In 1960, Evans's promotional literature glowed that the company's cycles would be "the showiest sidewalk bike in the neighborhood!" They certainly were, with their brightly striped seats, brilliant enameled finishes, "Buccaneer type" handlebars ("Kids go for their dashing appearance"), white-wall tires, and "deluxe chrome car-style fenders." The bikes even had a removable cross-piece to convert from a boy's to a girl's bike. "Here's a versatile 'family bike' that can be passed on from brother to sister or vice versa," the company said.

Evans also shrewdly caught the spirit of the times, combining military themes with a penchant for space-age imagery in naming its line: the Sky Cycle, with six models with names like the Defender and the Cadet.

In the mid-sixties, bicycle design made a radical change in appearance. Inspired by hot rod dragsters and the elongated front end of "chopper" motorcycles, manufacturers warped the long-standing symmetry of the basic bicycle and made it racier looking. Handlebars were stretched and bent into a severe U-shape with the handle grips bent down at the top. The wheels shrank, with the front wheel often smaller or thinner than the rear, which ballooned out into

thick, treadless drag-racer tires. And the seats flattened out and curved into a banana shape, attached to a chrome backrest-piece, which in some models lengthened into "sissy bars."

These speedy-looking new bikes also came with much more advanced gear systems than cycles had had before; the standard of the industry became a five-speed derailleur, preferably with shifting controls that looked like the stick shift knobs and T-bars used in drag racing automobiles. In 1969, Huffy took the auto references to their logical (or illogical) extreme, and replaced the handlebars on some high-rise models with a steering wheel.

Horns and bells were practical additions that helped riders negotiate bicycles amongst pedestrians. But the new, flashier bikes required sartorial splendor. To attract as much attention as possible, kids added weird accessories to enhance their "ride": a headlight that doubled as an emergency siren and flashing red light, various types of horns and bright vinyl streamers hanging out of the handle grips. An early favorite trick that didn't cost much was clothes-pinning playing (or baseball) cards to the tires, so they made an "engine" sound as the spokes turned and flapped the cards. Mattel capitalized on this penchant with V-Rroom!—a plastic battery-operated noisemaking "engine" that attached to any bike frame or came built-in to Mattel's own V-Rroom! line of bikes and tricycles.

The point of all this extravagance was that the appearance of speed was more important than actual cycling speed. As the kids grew older, though, cycling trends grew with them.

The ten-speed racing bike with handles that curled under to reduce riders' wind drag was manufactured through the sixties, but it didn't become the standard of the bike industry until the seventies, when baby boom kids had outgrown their wild banana seats and were looking for more practical styles. Those same consumers revived a flagging cycling industry in the mid-eighties when seemingly the entire generation decided racing speed was less important than the gear ratios, sturdy construction, and the wide, fat, trail-gripping features of mountain bikes.

JUMPING AROUND ON A POGO STICK NEVER GOT YOU VERY FAR, BUT KIDS WERE WILLING TO TRY ANYWAY.

STILTS' MAIN APPEAL FOR KIDS WAS PROBABLY THE ADDED HEIGHT—OTHERWISE, THEY WERE BORING.

## THE RIDE STUFF

We also grew up with alternative riding toys. Scooters have had occasional periods of popularity, and so have pogo sticks, which allow riders to hop until their brains churn themselves into gelatin. Jet Jumper sold its simple aluminum pogo stick in the mid-fifties. More than a decade later, the Master Pogo stick sported handlebars much like a bicycle's, and added a convenient feature for kids who felt compelled to compete over how many hops they'd taken: The Countmeter added each jump up to 9,999, but most kids got bored or fell off long before that.

The same company manufactured stilts, another item that enjoyed occasional resurgences. Most Boy Scout troops spent a lot of time and effort teaching boys how to make their own stilts with a few pieces of wood, but Master offered a clean, splinterless alternative with its Stilt Master, made of tubular steel finished in—what else?—a hot-rod red enamel.

In the early sixties, one riding fad caught on along California beaches: skateboards. In the almost three decades since the skateboard craze inspired Jan and Dean's "Sidewalk Surfing," the landlocked version of the surfboard has evolved into a product with amazingly complex details in wheel design, board shape, and composition unimaginable back when skateboards were simple flat pieces of wood mounted on modified roller-skate wheels.

The best part was that you didn't have to be two blocks from the ocean to be cool. It didn't matter if you were in Kansas City or Minneapolis, you could hang ten down the sidewalk to your best friend's driveway. There was that sense of freedom similar to learning to ride a bike, especially after you learned the trick of not falling on your butt. And once you learned the body English to stay on board, you were cool.

Like most fad items, skateboards went into hibernation until they were revived by punk high school boys in the late seventies and eighties. This time the association with surf music and crew cuts was gone— the music was speed metal or hardcore, the haircuts mohawks, and the boards' surfing logos were replaced with the skull and crossbones of the heavy metal cult.

Roller skates also underwent an evolutionary process in the past decades. In the fifties, skates were cumbersome steel armatures strapped to your feet with awkward tightening mechanisms adjusted with keys. Later, manufacturers such as Globe Fun Skates designed adjustable models that fastened without the easily lost keys. Another brand, Chicago, sold the even-more-comfortable Sneaker-Skate, which had the skate wheels preattached to canvas sneakers. These companies didn't fix one annoying thing about roller skates, though: Even into the late sixties, old-fashioned steel wheels were still standard equipment, and kids rattled their teeth loose even on the smoothest new suburban streets.

Most outdoor and riding toys were for warm-weather use. But one item has been a wintertime stalwart of the industry: the sled. And Blazon-Flexible Flyer is the most readily identifiable brand name in the history of sleds. The company was formed in 1889, but its history begins farther back than that.

Samuel Leeds Allen, a Pennsylvania Quaker businessman, left Philadelphia in 1861 to return to farming in New Jersey. In 1866, Allen invented two pieces of farm equipment, a fertilizer spreader and a seed drill. And by the late 1880s, his farm equipment factory was booming (Allen was a pioneer in such labor benefits as death and liability insurance, and retirement plans for his employees), but the business was seasonal. He

wanted to find a product he could make during the winter.

Allen had been tinkering around with sled designs to "coast" on the sloping hills around the family farm. After many false starts, he came up with a sled that had only one pair of steel runners, which could be steered via a hinged attachment halfway back. Allen called the sled the Flexible Flyer, and applied for a patent on Valentine's Day, 1889. The Flexible Flyer wasn't popular with retailers, so Allen shelved the idea.

In the early 1900s, he tried again, and this time, two major department stores, Wanamaker's in Philadelphia and Macy's in New York, stocked the sleds. The Flexible Flyer was a success at last—in 1915, Allen's company was selling two thousand sleds a day and overtook more established manufacturers, whose sleds couldn't be steered.

By the postwar era, Flexible Flyer had become the last word in sleds, and expanded its wintertime trade to Norwegian-style wooden skis. In 1968, the Allen company was sold to a conglomerate that merged Flexible Flyer with Blazon, makers of outdoor swing sets.

Other companies have tried their hand at matching Flexible Flyer: In the sixties, Withington pro-

IT DIDN'T MATTER IF YOU LIVED
NEAR A BEACH. BACKYARD
VINYL POOLS OFFERED THEIR
OWN OCEANS OF FUN.

duced the Jaguar, a children's version of its Bob-O-Link bobsleds (which has the four-ski configuration that Allen finally out-designed). And other kinds of sleds have taken their share of the market. Blazon (pre–Flexible Flyer merge) manufactured flat steel sleds, including a 1966 model that cashed in on the popularity of the "Batman" TV program, the Bat Wing. The Bat Wing was an aerodynamic-looking variation of the popular flying-saucer style of sled. The flying saucers were simple curved discs of aluminum with handles attached to the sides; kids would squat and hold on for dear life as they careened downhill out of control.

The seasonal flip side of sleds and other wintertime toys is the summertime favorite, the kids' backyard wading pool. The peculiar smell of warm water on fresh-from-the-factory vinyl lingered in the hot air, with bits of grass, dirt, and dead bugs floating amongst the frolicking children.

A number of manufacturers, as well as the catalog department stores, mass-produced the vinyl wading pools, which could be inflated, or the kind that hung on a tubular steel frame held down with bright plastic corner pieces that doubled as seats. Berle-Pinkerton Corporation's 1950 Vinylite Play Pools and Backyard Oceans helped set the standards. Though they were invariably only about a foot deep, they were advertised as "an innovation in summer comforts for the whole family." The Backyard Oceans line of frame pools even had a hose hookup that sprayed a fountain of water into the pool. The

## THE RIDE STUFF

Holiday Line was also a well-known pool maker, with its inflatable round vinyl wading pools.

Along with the pools came other ways to turn the garden hose into a toy to cool off with. Wham-O (FRISBEEs, Hula Hoops, and Super Balls) created the Water Wiggle, a wacky-looking plastic head that attached to the end of any hose and turned it into a wild, water-spraying snake that propelled itself willy-nilly as kids ran screaming for cover. Wham-O didn't stop there. The company also sold the Slip 'n Slide, a long bright yellow plastic strip that unrolled into the yard and attached to a hose at one end. Kids took a running start and leapt onto the slide—head-first, feet-first, whatever—and slipped all the way down the cool wet runway.

When manufacturers ran out of new gimmicks for the pools themselves, they concentrated on kids' furniture, like Moulded Products' Step 'n Slide (a twenty-inch one-piece mini-slide that's still sold today, that was the perfect size for toddlers to climb all over), and the Kiddy Kontour adjustable playchair, which could recline or rock to suit kids.

Kids' furniture was an extension of the market for backyard swing sets, one of the dependable moneymakers for toy stores. Though many companies offered various combinations of swing and slide sets based on playground-quality rides, few came up with novel designs like Gym Dandy's "Swing-sation of 1962," the Twirler. Universal Manufacturing, which had been making the Gym Dandy line since 1945, proudly announced that the Twirler, which hung alongside more conventional swings and seesaws, "spins like a top, orbits like a man in space, and swings at the same time."

Even backyard swing sets, just like bicycle and other riding designs, reflected society's obsessions at the time, whether it was sleeker, faster cars or swinging in outer space.

# Blinded by Science

In purely technological terms, the world, and especially the United States, changed profoundly after World War II. Though experiments had been going on for years, nuclear energy burst upon the public reality when the first nuclear weapon was detonated near Alamogordo, New Mexico, on July 16, 1945. The awesome power of the atomic age was etched upon the world the next month when the United States devastated Hiroshima and Nagasaki with two bombs, leading to the end of the war with Japan.

Technological advances fundamentally altered the shape of postwar American life-styles: in 1949 the first jet crossed the country in three hours and 46 minutes. Bell Laboratories' scientists discovered the transistor in 1947, one year before Peter Goldmark developed the long-playing record. Penicillin was first used to treat chronic diseases in 1943. The first contraceptive pill was produced in 1952. Transatlantic cable telephone service was inaugurated in 1958. The laser beam, which now serves as a "needle" to play your compact discs (which have replaced the long-playing record in less than half a century) and which surgeons use routinely for eye surgery, was developed in 1960.

Science was bustin' out all over. Perhaps just as important was for the first time we could see the changes as they happened—even nuclear bomb tests—in the comfort of our living rooms on television. Kids dreamed of rocketing to the moon during the forties and fifties; they watched men walk there by the end of the sixties.

ASIDE FROM ADDING CONTEMPORARY FLYING MACHINES LIKE SPACE SHUTTLES, GUILLOW'S HASN'T CHANGED THE DESIGNS OF ITS BEST-SELLING JET FIGHTERS SINCE THE KOREAN WAR.

Hope sprang eternal back then. The period from July 1, 1957, to December 31, 1958, was designated the International Geophysical Year, during which a worldwide systematic study of the earth and its environment was conducted that involved the cooperation of nearly seventy nations and thirty thousand scientists and observers in thousands of places from the equator to both poles. It was the first cooperative effort to study the planet, and significant discoveries like the Van Allen radiation belts surrounding the earth were made during the I.G.Y.

The space race, which eventually ended with the American manned moon landings from 1969 to 1972, was on when the Soviet Union sent up Sputniks I and II in 1957, in the midst of the I.G.Y. The satellites expanded the Cold War and terrified the rest of the world, especially the United States, in the process.

Our eyes were aimed skyward. First there were traditional toys celebrating flight, such as kites (one of the oldest of flying toys), then came the planes. Companies such as Guillow's supplied an endless stream of simple, guaranteed-to-last-for-at-least-several-flights balsa wood gliders.

Gas-powered scale-model planes came from manufacturers like Cox, and every conceivable aircraft from every era miniaturized in plastic by Revell, AMT, Aurora, and other model companies. Toy planes were stamped out in tin, plastic, and even inflatable vinyl.

But airplanes and jets somehow never allowed the imagination to soar as high as a rocket ship. The reality of mankind's technological prowess put the stars foremost in our dreams in the sixties; man was moving rapidly into space.

By 1948, rocket missiles reached speeds of three thousand miles an hour and altitudes of seventy-eight

miles above the earth. By the early fifties, both the United States and the Soviet Union were attempting to put satellites in orbit around the planet.

The fascination with space started long before the first men reached orbit. Any fan of Jules Verne knows that as far back as the 1800s—long before men could even fly—men were dreaming about ways to get to the moon.

Science fiction—that is, fiction written in response to the technological changes in the world—has been around, in one form or another, since the nineteenth century. (Many historians consider Mary Shelley's 1818 *Frankenstein* to be the first science fiction novel.) Both Verne and H. G. Wells enjoyed great popularity in the late nineteenth and early twentieth centuries with their novels about space travel and wars between alien worlds.

Pulp novels, named after the cheap pulp paper they were printed on, and which often featured colorful representations of space ships and foreign worlds on their covers, got started with *Argosy* in 1896, and publications like *Amazing Stories* and *Astounding Stories of Super Science* mixed science fiction plots among the Westerns and adventure stories in the thirties before World War II. *Amazing Stories* begat Buck Rogers in 1928.

By 1934 millions of American kids were zapping each other with their own Buck Rogers space pistol, sold by the Daisy Manufacturing Co., in an early display of the power of merchandising tie-ins. The same year Flash Gordon debuted, and both spawned their own toys: wagons shaped like rocket ships, watches, billfolds, metal figures, windup toys, ray guns, sonic air blasters, and rocket fighters.

Early television space programs in the fifties followed in Buck's and Flash's images. Working on low budgets, they nonetheless set the tone and established the images we grew up with.

Kids started taking after their televised heroes—"Captain Video," starring Al Hodge as a Flash Gordon–type good guy with wild weapons and costumes that looked more like forties detective movie rejects than futuristic apparel,

COX MAY BE THE NAME WE
REMEMBER BEST WHEN WE
THINK OF GAS-ENGINE PLANES,
BUT OTHER COMPANIES, SUCH
AS COMET, MADE THEIR OWN,
INCLUDING THIS U.S. AIR FORCE
SABRE 44.

appeared first in 1949, followed by "Tom Corbett, Space Cadet" (based on a story by Robert Heinlein, also a consultant to the program), "Captain Z-Ro," "Rod Brown of the Rocket Rangers," "Atom Squad," "Jet Jackson, Flying Commando," "Captain Midnight," "Commando Cody," "Space Patrol," and "Rocky Jones, Space Ranger."

All were characterized by the same cheap cardboard sets, way-out uniforms, and heroes who kept villains from taking over the earth and/or the universe. Scenes of rocket launchings were primitive at best, small models held by wires (that were clearly visible) taking off shakily into the sky. Even "Phantom Empire," a movie serial made in the thirties starring the famous cowboy Gene Autry and a futuristic city beneath the Earth, was resurrected on television for a new generation of children in the fifties.

Toy tie-ins helped make these programs' stars household names. Millions of kids drank Ovaltine from their special club mugs because Captain Midnight told them it was essential in the fight between good and evil in the interplanetary cosmos. What future astronaut could live without a Tom Corbett lunch

THE BUCK ROGERS SONIC RAY
GUN HELPED KEEP THE UNI-
VERSE SAFE IN 1954.

box, matching thermos, school bag or coloring book? Toys often reflected simplistic attitudes about space. Little space rangers ran around everywhere, and toy companies came up with products to help them play out their fantasies.

On TV in the sixties, Captain Midnight and Flash Gordon were replaced by adventure programs that were just as awkward-looking as their predecessors. The complex camera work didn't always hide the clumsy movements of the puppets and the tiny scale of the sets for such British-made series as "Fireball XL5" and "Stingray" (which took place underwater instead of in outer space). Later sci-fi television programs of the sixties included "Time Tunnel" and "Lost in Space."

The biggest space television program of all time was "Star Trek." Though the acting was no better than daytime soap operas and the sets not much of an improvement over the flimsy "Tom Corbett, Space Cadet" stages fifteen years earlier, the three years' worth of adventures in the galaxies of the starship *Enterprise* with Captain Kirk and his crew mesmerized—and continue to entrance—Trekkies.

BANNER PLASTICS CORPORATION'S 1955 SPACE HELMET HAD EYEPIECES THAT LOOKED SUSPICIOUSLY LIKE BADMINTON SHUTTLECOCKS. FASTEN YOUR SEAT BELTS, KIDS.

TO FIGHT IN THE SPACE AGE, EVERYTHING HAD TO LOOK AERODYNAMIC—EVEN DART AND WATER GUNS WERE SHAPED LIKE ROCKET SHIPS.

*Space patrol*

Manufacturers came up with Star Trek items by the dozens. The Star Trek Flashlite Ray Gun, made by Larami Incorporated, was a working flashlight emblazoned with the Star Trek insignia. The Star Trek binoculars were bright red and white and made you feel like you were on the deck of the Enterprise alongside Dr. Spock himself.

But "Star Trek" was ultimately only fantasy; the continuing American space program was reality.

The 1969 U.S. moon landing was an historic occasion, as the entire world watched Neil Armstrong and Buzz Aldrin leaping around in their moon boots. It was a dream come true, and toy manufacturers leaped into the fray with toys based on the real-life astronauts. The best space toys were produced by Japanese manufacturers, and none of the astronaut items was as sleek as the science fiction fantasies of the thirties and forties, but rather functional in design and appearance.

Manufacturers such as Centuri supplied hobbyists with rockets, but Estes Industries, a company started with the express purpose of creating high-powered rockets that burned prepacked fuel canisters, was the leader in model rocketry.

The company had its roots in the postwar effort to develop space technology. Estes designed its earliest model rockets as exact replicas of ones being made for the U.S. space program, a practice Estes still follows today (the company now sells working replicas of the space shuttles, which separate from their rocket halves and fly back to earth, just like the real thing). The model rocket industry takes itself quite seriously—the National Association of Rocketry even has a fourteen-point safety code, which proudly accounts for the more than 300 million successful model rocket launches since the hobby was established.

But rocket models are more complicated than toy rockets. For kids who weren't interested in dealing with the careful setup and detonation, as well as the packing of the parachutes (to retrieve your rocket once it spent its payload), there certainly were plenty of other ways to fantasize about space.

One was to see the space program unfold in three-dimensional glory, right before your eyes. All it took was a View-Master, a disarmingly simple device that allowed kids to see various stories in 3-D slide form. The Sawyer family, which invented the View-Master, started a photographic developing company in the early 1900s. The family came up with the idea to create a mass-produced stereo slide scope based on a primitive stereo photograph viewer. The View-Master was first introduced at the 1939 New York World's Fair, and though the viewers have been redesigned since then, those original reels can still be used today.

In the mid-fifties, reels afforded 3-D peeks not only on scientific topics, but also travel

ASIDE FROM THE STAR TREK NAME AND LOGO, THERE WASN'T ANYTHING HI-TECH ABOUT LARAMI'S FLASHLITE RAY GUN AND BINOCULARS, "THE ONLY OFFICIALLY-LICENSED BINOCULARS WITH ALL THE APPEAL OF ONE OF THE MOST POPULAR SHOWS ON TELEVISION!"

## BLINDED BY SCIENCE

IT DIDN'T TAKE LONG FOR COMPANIES TO ADD SPACESHIP MODELS ALONGSIDE THEIR CARS AND BOATS, AS MAN HEADED FOR THE MOON.

(states, foreign countries, and tourist attractions were highlighted in multiple-reel packets), famous events (how about the 1955 Miss America pageant, or Eisenhower's inauguration?), famous people ("Baseball Stars") and nature ("Wonders of the Deep," "San Diego Zoo, California"), in addition to the real draw for kids: story and adventure packets (Disney movies, *20,000 Leagues Under the Sea*) and cartoons.

In a stroke of genius, a slew of well-known characters from movies, television, books, and comics, were licensed for the reels. By the end of the sixties, you could even enjoy a Peanuts story told with dolls.

GAF, the company that took over the toy, later created a Talking View-Master which brought the cartoon reels to life. The original design used a small record attached to the

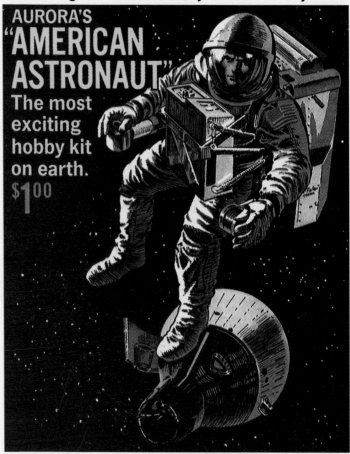

**Now being launched at hobby counters everywhere**

AURORA'S "AMERICAN ASTRONAUT" The most exciting hobby kit on earth. $1.00

reels, so the viewers were bulky, but hearing the voices of Yogi Bear and Boo-Boo beat seeing comic book conversation bubbles above the 3-D scenes. The company also made a Talking View-Master Electronic Lighted Stereo Viewer. That last was a mouthful to say, but it was a simple evolution for the View-Master: instead of having to crane your neck toward a window or a lamp, a switch turned on an enclosed tiny light bulb that illuminated the reels.

Mixed media also were sold to kids with a surprising array of semi-sophisticated projectors, many made by Kenner, that allowed kids to hang a sheet on the wall and

137

hold screenings of comics transferred to strips of cartoon slides. The Give-A-Show Projector was popular throughout the late sixties, with an extensive selection of shows that could be viewed. Each Give-A-Show refill set contained five different "shows" on thirty-five color slides, including ones starring the exciting new breed of superheroes who proliferated in comic books.

The sixties was the decade when comic-book characters first were raised to a social phenomenon. Half science fiction and half trashy pulp narratives, comic books brought to life fantasy superheroes that outdid the brave astronauts in amazing feats for the good of mankind.

The roots of the superhero phenomenon were planted in the thirties, when characters such as Superman (1938) and Batman (1939) were first inked in the pages of comic books. Along with such mysterious heroes as the Shadow, Superman and Batman jumped media onto the radio airwaves. In the fifties, Superman made the more crucial jump, to television. Batman waited until 1966; the Shadow had already slipped into the darkness.

"The Adventures of Superman" was one of the most popular and enduring of the early TV sci-fi showcases; the program was an immediate hit when it debuted in the fall of 1952. The instantly recognizable introduction for the series says it all: "Faster than a speeding bullet!" an overeager narrator yelled out of the TV. "More powerful than a locomotive! Able to leap tall buildings at a single bound!"

"Look! Up in the sky!" an onlooker yelled. "It's a bird! It's a plane! It's ... Superman!"

AMSCO'S ALPHA-1 BALLISTIC MISSILE (WITH REMOTE LAUNCHING PAD) USED COMPRESSED AIR OR WATER TO PROPEL ITSELF INTO THE SKY. THE COMPANY CLAIMED IT WAS "DESIGNED BY MISSILE ENGINEERS AND TESTED AT CAPE CANAVERAL."

## BLINDED BY SCIENCE

STYLED TO LOOK LIKE SPACE-AGE BINOCULARS, THE VIEW-MASTER OFFERED A 3-D PEEK AT THE WORLD.

KENNER'S GIVE-A-SHOW PROJECTOR WAS A KIDS' VERSION OF AN OVERHEAD PROJECTOR. BUT INSTEAD OF THE EDUCATIONAL PROGRAMS YOU'D SEE AT SCHOOL, KENNER OFFERED TV CARTOON HEROES FROM FAMILIAR CHARACTERS LIKE SPIDERMAN AND SUPERMAN TO LATE-SIXTIES CHARACTERS LIKE ATOM ANT AND SECRET SQUIRREL.

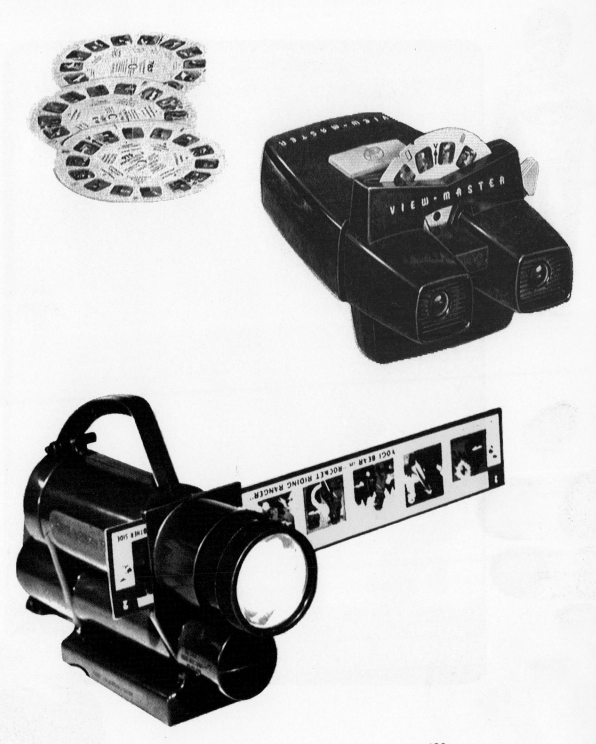

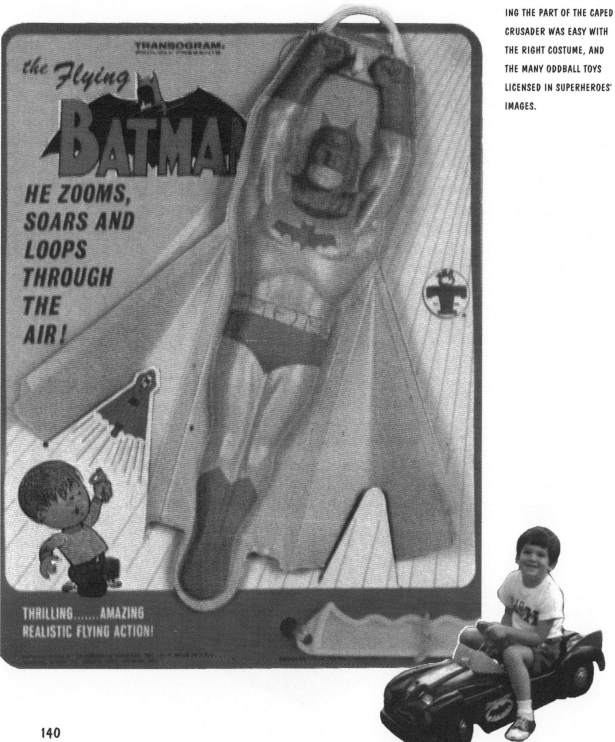

HOLY HERO WORSHIP! PLAYING THE PART OF THE CAPED CRUSADER WAS EASY WITH THE RIGHT COSTUME, AND THE MANY ODDBALL TOYS LICENSED IN SUPERHEROES' IMAGES.

With such an urgent call, how could Superman lose? Despite their simplistic story lines (repackaged cowboy or gangster plots with an outer-space twist) and primitive set designs, the shows added fuel to the fantasy fires already burning in the brains of kids dreaming of outer space denizens in remote galaxies. Superman was a big hit with toy manufacturers, too, because they could tie in with merchandising, starting at the very basic fantasy level of costumes for little boys to dress up like the Man of Steel.

A. C. Gilbert capitalized on Superman-mania by using the hero as the company's tireless promoter. Gilbert's 1948 catalog used Superman throughout, leading a tour of the Gilbert Hall of Science. "Railroading is full of thrilling action and spectacular drama," he announces to a couple of kids gawking at a train set.

But the Superman phenomenon was nothing compared to what would happen to his caped ally in the sixties. Let's face it, the Man of Steel had superpowers—he didn't need fancy gadgets to do his superwork, which frustrated toy makers.

Which is where Batman, a costumed human hero who relied on crimefighting gimmickry, came in. In 1966, a campy version of the Batman comics set toy manufacturers scrambling for a piece of the action, just as they were gearing up for the long haul with spy toys.

If "The Adventures of Superman" was the perfect TV embodiment of fifties American society, "Batman" was just as apt for the sixties: It was irreverent, campy to a fault, and chock-full of pop-art references. After each cliffhanger ending (the show aired in two parts on Wednesday and Thursday nights), the announcer invited viewers to tune in, "same time, same channel," to find out how everything worked out the next night.

One highlight of the program was the crazy graphics that flashed onscreen during the fight scenes. The show was a spoof, though its spin-off toys were taken very seriously by manufacturers. And the characters themselves were taken to heart by the kids who were enthralled by Batman—in the mid-sixties, adults were polarized by all the turbulent changes society was undergoing, but youngsters could seek solace in the silliness of the Batman myth.

Other popular superheroes of the day, who also made their way onto toy shelves in various incarnations, like science fiction movies of the fifties and sixties, all had direct links to science—most often, science gone berserk. Spiderman was bitten by a radioactive spider (it had been exposed during a nuclear experiment); the Incredible Hulk, a popular source for seventies toys when the character hit the TV screen in a series starring Bill Bixby, was a scientist who accidentally was exposed during a radioactive "cobalt bomb" test detonation; the Fantastic Four were given their strange superhuman powers when they were on an experimental space flight buffeted by a radioactive shower; the X-Men were the mutant crime-fighting offspring of human parents. The Silver Surfer was an alien (who rode a space-age surfboard through the galaxies, no less) banished to earth by his master, the planet-eating Galacticus, because he felt compassion for earthlings and rebelled when Galacticus wanted to feast on the planet's energy.

In 1966, Ideal went so far as to create a multiple-personality superhero doll modeled on the successful G.I. Joe. Captain Action, as he was called in his out-of-the-box state, was a generic do-gooder in a quasi-military costume, with a lightning-bolt-shaped sword in one rigid hand and a futuristic pistol in the other.

Instead of creating an array of fantasy situations and accessories for Captain Action, who was "spearheading the thundering wave of popularity and interest in superheroes," Ideal designed a complement of masks and other costumes to convert Captain Action into nine other, already familiar figures. He could switch into traditional human heroes like the Lone Ranger, Flash Gordon, Steve Canyon, or Sgt. Fury (a comic-book Army character), as well as superhuman good guys: Aquaman, Captain America, the Phantom, Batman, and Superman. Now, kids could save the world—or, at least, their parents' living room—nine different ways. After all, there was no resting when it came to being vigilant about evil.

Mattel created its own doll based on G.I. Joe, Major Matt Mason, a cross between a fighting soldier and a superhero. Introduced in 1966, Mason was a sci-fi astronaut, who presaged the Apollo moon landing with an all-terrain Space Crawler, a Space Sled, Space Station, and a Moon Suit. The doll was advertised on TV and in comic books—complete with a brief comic story in a two-page spread.

When they weren't lost in space or caught up in superhero fantasies, science toys took on more practical dimensions.

Erector was created by A. C. Gilbert, then owner of the Mysto Manufacturing Co., which sold professional magic equipment. Gilbert got the idea in 1911 while traveling on an electric rail line from his company's headquarters in New Haven, Connecticut. He watched the construction of the lines with fascination, especially the building of the steel girders that would serve as inspiration for his building sets.

In 1913, after a couple of years of experimentation, Gilbert introduced his Erector set. That year the company, soon to be renamed the A. C. Gilbert Company, grossed $141,000 and made a tidy profit in the process. It didn't take long for Erector to become part of the vernacular of young boys around the country, as they began constructing Ferris wheels, airplanes, trains, merry-go-rounds, dirigibles, parachute jumps, magnetic cranes, bridges, and pumps

with steel girders, wheels, nuts and bolts. They either followed the included instructions or created their own designs in response to Gilbert's endless contests for owners' models. Winners would get their design included in instruction books.

After World War II, Erector added remote control motors, as well as an Electric Amusement Park Set, which built a Parachute Jump and Merry-Go-Round. With the Electric Engine Set, kids could build the Airplane Ride and Windmill, while the cheaper, more basic Professional Set made a hoist and an elevator.

Erector sets attracted some notable fans over the years. Gilbert can count astronaut John Glenn and presidents John F. Kennedy, Jimmy Carter, and Ronald Reagan among its "master builders."

Many Erector sets were used in other model apparatuses. The Erector Whistle Kit, for instance, could be used with trains (Gilbert made American Flyer Trains, too), and an early fifties Erector set called the Smoke and Choo-Choo Kit was the smoke-in-tender unit for the popular steam locomotives that helped boost train sales in the postwar period.

Gilbert was in the forefront of scientific toy makers who kept up with the advances of the fifties. A 1959 Gilbert catalog includes the Space Age Erector set, which contained cut-out plastic parts to enable junior erectors to build missiles, rockets, and jets and take them apart within seconds without glue or cement. It listed for $3.98. The Fun With Electricity set came with equipment to build a rheostat and telegraph and perform more than fifty electrical and magnetic experiments, all for $9.98. Another more elaborate Physics Lab allowed little scientists to experiment with solar heat, air and water pressure, and bending light.

As with train sets, during the space age the popularity of Erector sets declined, although new ideas, like the Military Vehicles and Road Building Equipment sets, were still being introduced as late as 1965. Another 1965 innovation, a Ride-'em Erector that created life-size riding toys, failed.

Though it tried to make its products as up-to-date as possible, the company itself was woefully outdated in its marketing and production technology. By the mid-sixties, Gilbert had added a host of novelty and fad toys in an effort to catch up, even licensing a number of toys tied into TV series such as "The Man from U.N.C.L.E." and the popular movie spy, James Bond. But it was too little too late, and even its attempts at being trendy failed.

Gilbert declared bankruptcy in 1966, an ironic end to a company that had built its reputation on toys of the future. Observers noted that when the

company went under, the last blow was delivered by the dismal failure of its extravagant James Bond 007 Road Race Set, a slot-car set complete with a preformed mountain landscape and complex features. After several changes in corporate ownership, the View-Master Ideal Co. (the giants had formed one corporation and bought out Gilbert) discontinued Erector sets completely in 1988, citing the total saturation of the building market by LEGO.

Television helped promote science to children. "Watch Mr. Wizard," which first aired in 1951, starred Don Herbert as an avuncular neighbor who amazed kids with on-screen experiments using common household items. Besides repeating those simple experiments, kids could buy kits that distilled basic principles into tidy, learn-as-you-play packages in the fields of biology, chemistry, electronics, astronomy, and even weather forecasting.

The most popular such kits—which parents were always eager to buy in the hopes their kids would grow up to be respected scientists—were the various brands of microscopes and the myriad experiments you could observe with them. Gilbert, Skil-Craft, and Porter (makers of the Chemcraft and Microcraft lines) were busy assembling ever more complex microscope sets, with multiple turrets for different-powered viewing, and more and more different kinds of samples to stare at. The 650-power Gilbert Professional Microscope & Lab Set came complete with dried shrimp eggs that could be hatched, all under your scrutiny, with the baby shrimp swimming around the glass slide after only fifteen to twenty hours. When you got bored with the samples provided by the company, you could find plenty of your own to study: plants, boogers, dirt, hair, sugar granules, pieces of skin, ants, spiders, and

MODEL HOBBYISTS COULD TURN TO SCIENTIFIC CREATIONS, INCLUDING THE FAMOUS "VISIBLE" FIGURES THAT SHOWED HUMAN ANATOMY; THEY COULD ALSO ASSEMBLE ITC'S GIGANTIC BUMBLEBEE.

even the tiny living creatures in water samples from the muddy pond nearby.

The chemistry sets were almost as involved. They started out with simple experiments, such as mixing vinegar and baking soda together and watching the mixture foam. But they also got much more complex, setting the stage for later when you'd be forced to take chemistry in high school.

One of the most amazing science "fads" of the late fifties was the inclusion of nuclear energy experiments in chemistry sets of the day. Gilbert's Atomic Chemistry Laboratory boasted that it included "all the supplies and equipment you need to perform 1000 experiments. Imagine being able to watch harmless radio-active materials ... the disintegration of atomic particles!" The set didn't come with a Geiger counter, unfortunately. Chemcraft's Senior Lab also included atomic experiments, which you could presumably test on the included "uranium ore." The company assured its customers, though, that "these Chemcraft sets contain no dangerous poisons or explosive chemicals."

FUTURE DISC JOCKEYS COULD BUILD THEIR OWN TUBE RADIO RECEIVERS, WHICH BROADCAST OUT OF TABLE RADIOS WITHIN A FIFTY-FOOT RANGE.

FOR LESS THAN $10 IN 1957, ASPIRING ASTRONOMERS HAD A CHANCE TO PEER THROUGH A TINY 1¾-INCH LENS AT THE MOON AND STARS.

Still, these kits were important introductions for budding brainiacs. The kids who were hooked by them could go on and develop their affinity for the sciences throughout school, and contribute to that technology as adults.

Scientific "toys" were available everywhere, it seemed. In the backs of comic books and *Boys' Life* magazines, fascinating items were advertised every month. You could order amazing Sea Monkeys; plastic undersea

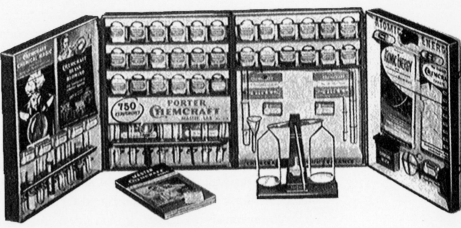

frogmen with tanks that you filled with baking soda (for the bubble effect); a cardboard, sort-of-life-sized submarine; "100 Individual Magnets, all Brand-New, only 79 cents Postpaid"; and the mysterious X-Ray Spex.

Live Pet Seahorses arrived at your door for 75 cents ("Live delivery guaranteed!"), Darling Pet Monkeys for $15 ("Eats same food as you, even likes lollipops"), Chik-Bator (an incubator complete with six quail eggs), dinosaur bone collections, and a treasure trove of scientific gewgaws (giant eight- or sixteen-foot weather balloons, "Great backyard fun. Exciting Beach attraction").

Also found in comics was an order form for Edmund Scientific's catalog, where many a budding scientist found solace. Edmund supplied scientific items for use in schools, universities, and industrial laboratories, and also included industrial giants like RCA, General Electric, General Motors, Philco, and Boeing on their client list. The catalog was heaven for young brains. Where else could you find underwater ant cities, crystal growing kits,

THE STILL-POPULAR GIANT ANT FARM TURNED THE WONDERS OF MOTHER NATURE INTO A PLAYTHING—ALBEIT AN EDUCATIONAL ONE.

magnetism kits, atomic gardening kits, or molecular model kits so you could compete in the science fair to get a decent grade from your teacher?

With the information age just around the corner, communication technology also crept into playthings. Walkie-talkies came in models as diverse as the Roy Rogers Western-style phones to the more modern-looking plastic sets, although both allowed you to talk with your best friend at the other end of the block. Amateur broadcasting sets mimed ham operators, a telegraph set clicked out messages in Morse code.

Mock electronic science setups were popular, too, with instrument panels so you could operate your own civil defense center, radarscope, or jet aircraft. The Radar Rocket Cannon spotted planes on its radarscope and put a flying rocket at your fingertips when you decided to fire away. The Radio Station had a revolving searchlight above its dials and gauges, and included an automatic Morse code selector dial. The Radar Defense Center was even fancier, with antennae that moved up and down. An identification screen and friend-foe lever helped you decide whether to shoot the approaching aircraft out of the sky. An enclosed map got your friends involved, plotting positions of planes on the radarscope, just like in the movie *Fail-Safe*.

REMCO, A FAMILIAR COMPANY THROUGH THE FIFTIES AND SIXTIES, MADE A SERIES OF WAR TOYS, INCLUDING THE RADAR ROCKET CANNON. THE TWENTY-INCH CONSOLE, COMPLETE WITH A GLOWING RADAR SCREEN, A SPINNING ANTENNA, AND A WORKING ROCKET LAUNCHER, TURNED A DEN INTO COMMAND CENTRAL.

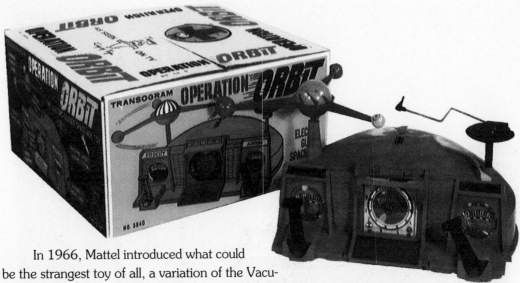

In 1966, Mattel introduced what could
be the strangest toy of all, a variation of the Vacu-
form, a waffle iron–like machine with a pump handle which melted smelly
sheets of plastic around simple molds. The onslaught began with an electric
heating element Mattel called the Thingmaker and a sludgy solution called Plastigoop. Kids could make their own plastic toys by pouring goop into
prestamped molds and heating it until it hardened. Some of the Thingmaker
packs Mattel created included relatively commonplace toys such as miniature
soldiers. The Fighting Men set made "bendable soldiers in permanent plastic!
Combat and field equipment too!"

But Mattel designers also stretched their imaginations and came up with
some truly original, bizarre creations: Creeple Peeple were wacked-out creatures with faces like the familiar (and ugly) troll dolls, and bodies straight out of
some sci-fi comic. Creepy Crawlers were molds of a variety of insects and other
scary, slimy things, from flies to spiders. The company even sold a Batman's
Bat Maker-Pak so kids could mold their own tiny bats.

The next year, Mattel added Fright Factory, which allowed kids to make
hideous monster-makeup items—scars, fangs, claws that fit over your fingertips, and a huge bloodshot eye. It was the perfect gift if your birthday fell just
before Halloween.

Also in 1967, during the Summer of Love, Mattel unveiled Incredible Edibles, made with an edible (though not necessarily digestible) version of Plasti-
goop. The company proudly exclaimed: "They're incredible because they
come in the form of (ugh!) spiders. And (ulp!) caterpillars. And (awk!) snakes.

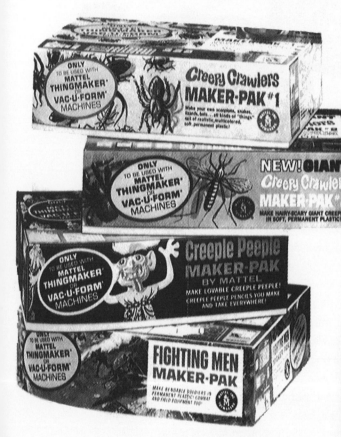

MATTEL CREATED THE WEIRDEST TOY SENSATION EVER WITH ITS THINGMAKER SERIES, WHICH INCLUDED KITS LIKE CREEPLE PEEPLE AND CREEPY CRAWLERS. USING THE COMPANY'S PLASTI-GOOP, KIDS COULD MAKE THEIR ROOMS INTO A SPAWNING GROUND FOR RUBBERY CREATURES.

IT WAS EASY TO GROSS OUT GROWN-UPS BY SWALLOWING THE REALISTIC SNAKES AND BUGS CREATED BY MATTEL'S INCREDIBLE EDIBLES KITS. THE SYRUP THAT HARDENED INTO THE MOLDS WAS SO PURE, THE COMPANY INSISTED, THAT IT EARNED THE GOOD HOUSEKEEPING SEAL OF APPROVAL.

WITH THE THINGMAKER FRIGHT FACTORY, YOU COULD MAKE YOURSELF INTO THE GHOUL NEXT DOOR FOR HALLOWEEN. THE "GENUINE PLASTIGOOP" SOLD BY MATTEL COULD BE MOLDED INTO AWFUL MONSTER-MAKEUP ADDITIONS, WHICH YOU LICKED AND STUCK ON YOUR FACE.

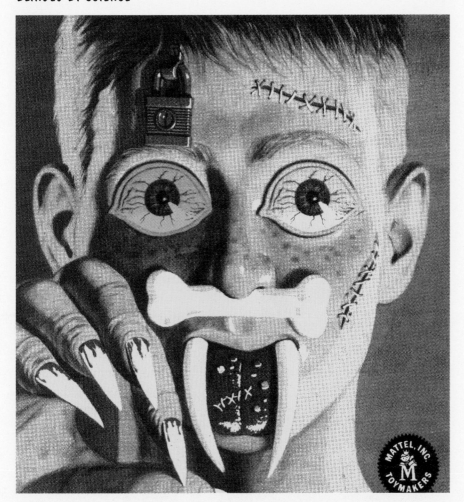

And (urp!) assorted other bugs and insects. And kids love 'em. Of course, they're not *real* bugs and insects. They're like Creepy Crawlers, made out of candy. Candy the kids can make themselves. Candy that looks horrible, but tastes great." Tell that to any kid who tried to down a root beer–flavored rubbery snake.

Mattel continued to introduce heat-activated novelties into 1968, when the company introduced its Time Machine, which took innocuous plastic squares with the Mattel logo on them and changed them inside a heated chamber into an assortment of strange, prehistoric creatures. The heat simply made the square pieces unfold—you could then squish them into a compressor, and they popped back out in their original square form.

With this toy, Mattel had competition. Wham-O came out the same year with its Shrink Machine, which created solid miniature toys out of larger pieces of plastic. You colored an image on a Shrink Machine sheet, then cut it out and placed it in the gadget. As it shrank, it got thicker, so at the end, you had a solid, if not quite three-dimensional, toy to show for all your trouble.

ROBOTS CAME IN ALL DIFFERENT SHAPES AND SIZES. SOME WERE SHAPED LIKE ANIMALS OR SPACE BUSES; ONE BATTERY-POWERED ROBOT EVEN CAME WITH ITS OWN BABY.

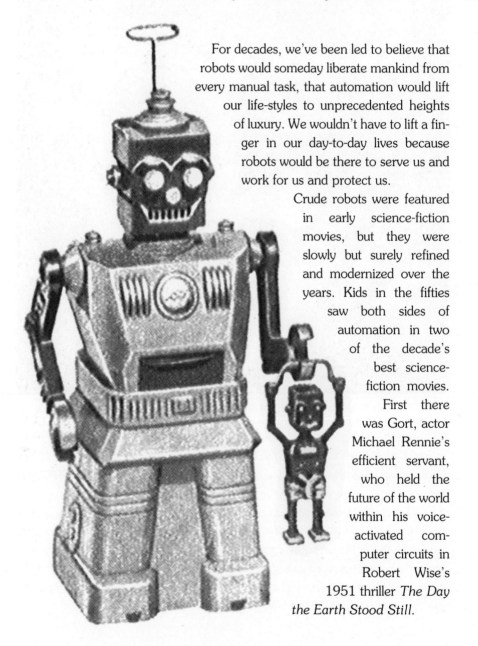

For decades, we've been led to believe that robots would someday liberate mankind from every manual task, that automation would lift our life-styles to unprecedented heights of luxury. We wouldn't have to lift a finger in our day-to-day lives because robots would be there to serve us and work for us and protect us.

Crude robots were featured in early science-fiction movies, but they were slowly but surely refined and modernized over the years. Kids in the fifties saw both sides of automation in two of the decade's best science-fiction movies. First there was Gort, actor Michael Rennie's efficient servant, who held the future of the world within his voice-activated computer circuits in Robert Wise's 1951 thriller *The Day the Earth Stood Still.*

And then there was Robbie, a combination R2D2 and C3PO that faithfully served Walter Pidgeon and Anne Francis on the planet Altair-4 in Fred M. Wilcox's *Forbidden Planet.* More often than not, robots were caricatured as helpful rather than destructive, culminating with the robots in the *Star Wars* films.

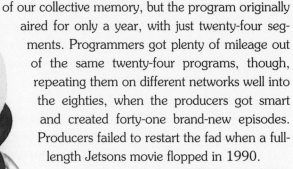

By the time "The Jetsons," the camp sci-fi cartoon, first aired in September of 1962, the idea of a future with robots for servants was not only believable, it seemed just around the corner. Push a button and your food would be cooked and served in an instant; the mechanical "maid" (Knickerbocker sold a marionette replica of Rosie, the robot maid) would follow after you with your pipe and slippers, or push the vacuum cleaner around the house. "The Jetsons" (along with its prehistoric counterpart, "The Flintstones") is a vivid part of our collective memory, but the program originally aired for only a year, with just twenty-four segments. Programmers got plenty of mileage out of the same twenty-four programs, though, repeating them on different networks well into the eighties, when the producers got smart and created forty-one brand-new episodes. Producers failed to restart the fad when a full-length Jetsons movie flopped in 1990.

And long before R2D2 and C3PO helped Luke Skywalker and Princess Leia save the Empire in *Star Wars,* a robot companion was one of the most popular "stars" of "Lost in Space," which aired from 1965 to 1968. The program followed the adventures of the space family Robinson as its members wandered the galaxies trying to get back to earth. The family's friendly robot (loosely based on *Forbidden Planet*'s Robbie) was a boxy machine that rolled along on tanklike treads and spent much of its time warning the Robinsons of trouble ahead by yelling, "Danger! Danger!"

Toy manufacturers wasted no time creating replicas of the show's robot. The series also spawned Mattel's Lost in Space Roto-Jet Gun, an interplanetary weapons system with four plastic missiles which made a shrieking wwheeeeeeeeee sound when they were fired.

Ideal's Mr. Machine was a benign figure that took toy stores by storm in the early sixties. Made of see-through plastic that showed off its oversized inner workings of brightly colored gears, nuts and bolts, Mr. Machine made noise and traveled across the floor with a few twists of the windup key in his back. As an educational extra, the robot could be taken apart piece by piece and reassembled.

The later Robert the Robot was a bit more complex; it came with a remote control that connected the robot through a wire, and Robert could move forward or backward and shoot missiles hidden in his head. There have been other robots of varying sizes and complexities sold through the years that have entertained kids briefly before heading into the junkheap of all used-up and broken toys. Ideal's King Zor, a scary, bulbous-eyed monster that resembled Godzilla, a creation of the sci-fi-crazed animators in Japan, lumbered around the room and roared while it shot plastic balls out of an opening in its green back. But most other robots were anonymous plastic creatures made to look like humanoid steel behemoths.

An early Electronic Brain was shaped like a space man in a car. Called Z-Man and offered in the Sears catalog, the foot-long robot car moved in different directions, fired missiles, and rounded obstacles with a preset "brain" that the owner programmed. Z-Man wound his way around the house on two battery-operated motors and cost $10.95.

By the seventies, with the exception of the mega-successful *Star Wars* characters, Americans had tired of robots. It was painfully obvious by then that we'd all still have to do our own chores, and home robotics was farther away than we thought.

Robots made a comeback in the mid-eighties, when TV introduced Transformers and Gobots, cars, trucks, planes, and rockets that transformed themselves into robot superheroes. The toy versions of these characters were ingeniously designed to "transform" themselves with just a few twists of the hand.

## BLINDED BY SCIENCE

YOU COULDN'T HOOK UP A JOYSTICK TO THEM, BUT THANKS TO EDMUND SCIENTIFIC'S MAIL ORDER CATALOGS, TECHNOLOGY-MINDED HOBBYISTS GOT AN EARLY INTRODUCTION TO HOME COMPUTERS.

At the same time that Transformers were taking over Saturday morning cartoons, a new breed of working robots briefly became the rage of well-to-do toy fans. These large "toys" (they looked like converted canister vacuum cleaners) could cost upwards of several hundred dollars, and could be remote-controlled to roll through the house carrying drinks or hors d'oeuvres.

Even in adulthood, science toys fascinate us—for a few months at least, the new wave of robots was a novel way to break the ice at yuppie cocktail parties.

### LEARN FIRSTHAND WHAT MAKES THE GIANT COMPUTERS TICK...SOLVE REAL PROBLEMS

It's fun. This new working model computer is a junior mechanical version of the electronic brains now used in modern business. Developed by two of the nation's foremost authorities in the field, it is capable of adding, subtracting and multiplying. It shifts, complements, carries, memorizes, counts, compares and sequences. With it you can play games, tell fortunes and challenge the imaginations of everyone in the family. Easy to assemble from rigid plastic parts in attractive colors. 12" long x 3½" wide x 4¾" high. Includes assembly diagrams plus 32-page manual covering operation, computer language (binary system), programming, problems and 15 experiments.

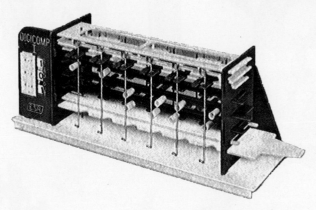

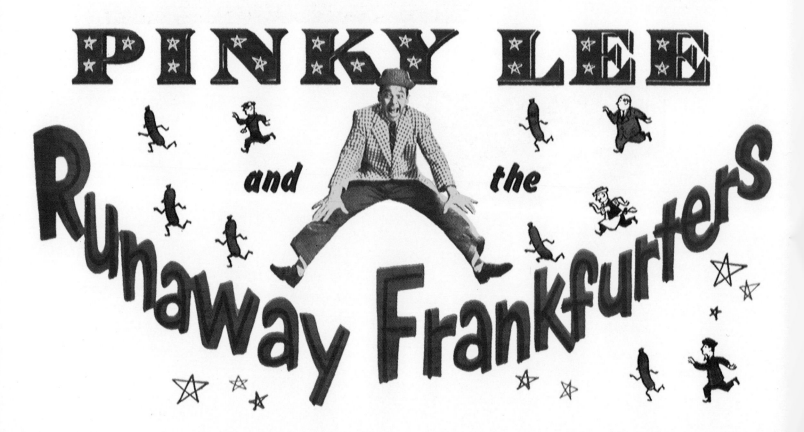

PINKY LEE and the Runaway Frankfurters

# Games People Play

**W**e've been playing games forever. Sports, competition, games, and contests have been as integral a part of our experience as eating, sleeping, or watching television.

    The first game boards were probably lines drawn in the ground, with bones, rocks, stones, or shells as pieces, used by adults or children repeating age-old rites of religion or magic. The origins of ancient games like backgammon and chess are clouded in mystery, but they have survived through the centuries and remain popular today.

    Three games of senet, similar to our present-day snakes and ladders game, were found in King Tut's tomb along with his jeweled mummy, and a game called hounds and jackals dates back to the twelfth dynasty in ancient Egypt. A diagram for nine-men's morris was found engraved on the steps of a Cretan temple.

    In their purest form, games allow the opportunity to imitate or fantasize about great battles and conquests, rule dynasties, buy vast amounts of real

**THE KID WITH THE STRAIGHTEST-SHOOTING THUMB WAS THE KING OF THE BLOCK WHEN IT CAME TO MARBLES.**

estate, and enjoy watching your opponent crawl before you in defeat—if you're lucky.

Games fall into three basic categories: skill, chance, and strategy. The rules can be decided upon beforehand or made up during play (everybody's made on-the-spot judgment calls). Many games can be played alone—solitaire, jacks, marbles, golf—but most are played with or against other people. Now they can be played against computer programs. Often, as with sports, games are played for the benefit of spectators as well as of the competitors themselves.

Marbles may be an ancient game, but they were never played as often as during the fifties and sixties, when battles for king-of-the-block were fought with sure-shooting thumbs and a supply of reliable cat's eyes, rainbows, moonies, marine puries, and jumbo shooters. One of the biggest manufacturers of marbles, not surprisingly, was called Marble King. Its parent company, Berry Pink Industries of New York, began making the glass balls during the twenties. Amsco even marketed a Marble Raceway in the sixties, for those bored with shooting them on the ground.

Not just glass balls, but balls of every type are part of growing up. Many childhood games—kickball, tetherball, foursquare—as well as a slew of adult sports—baseball, golf, and so on—depend on a wide array of specialty balls. One of the biggest manufacturers of balls over the years was Fli-Back, whose paddleball sets had plywood paddles silkscreened with oddly out-of-date graphics, and a rubber band stapled to the wood and a rubber ball at the other end.

The company also sold batons, tops, yo-yos, and rubber, vinyl, and plastic balls of all sizes, patterns, and colors. An earlier brand, Dewey and Almy Chemical Company's Darex playballs, came in Day-Glo (the word was registered by the company in the early fifties!) colors, and its largest size inflated to a truly awesome forty inches high.

As the sixties drew to a close, the ball was reinvented one more

DAREX'S 1952 DAY-GLO LINE
OF BALLS CAME IN SIZES UP
TO A GIANT FORTY INCHES.

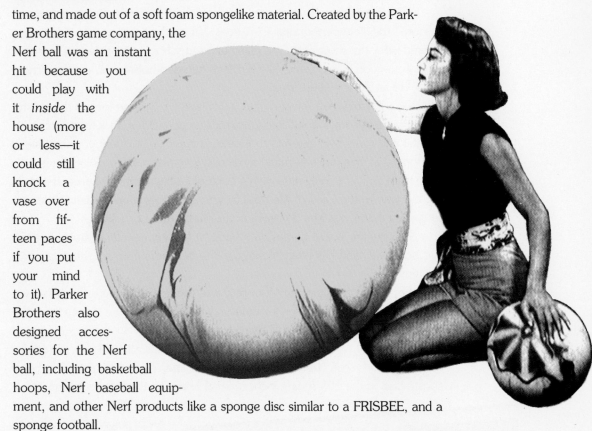

time, and made out of a soft foam spongelike material. Created by the Parker Brothers game company, the Nerf ball was an instant hit because you could play with it *inside* the house (more or less—it could still knock a vase over from fifteen paces if you put your mind to it). Parker Brothers also designed accessories for the Nerf ball, including basketball hoops, Nerf baseball equipment, and other Nerf products like a sponge disc similar to a FRISBEE, and a sponge football.

One last ball, which wasn't a bouncing ball at all, has been a popular seller since its introduction in the early fifties. The Magic "8" Ball was originally manufactured and sold by Alabe Crafts Inc., but it's since been taken over by the Ideal Corporation.

The "8" Ball has been a steady seller over the years despite, or quite possibly because of, its essential simplicity. The plastic ball, silkscreened with a billiard ball–style "8" on top, is filled with a dark blue-tinted liquid, with a window on its base to peer into the murk. The holder asks a question and turns the ball over to gaze into the window; an answer, one side of a multi-faceted piece etched with generic fortunes, appears out of the blue into the window.

But what first come to mind when people think of games are the ones played on boards. The Milton Bradley Company uses a five-question test for board games: Is it fun to play? Is there a reward? Is it challenging? Is it non-frustrating? Does it have "repeat-play value"?

Toy companies have always marketed board games during a "second season," the slow period after Christmas. When the temperature is hovering around zero, the snow outside is piling up, and school is canceled for a couple of days, a good board game, like a doll or gun-and-holster set, can become a kid's—or an adult's—best friend.

Board games can simulate real life or fantasy. No one forgets the satisfying feeling that comes when someone lands on your Boardwalk monopoly with a hotel and forks over the two thousand smackers—or offers you the yellow monopoly at bargain basement rates trying to keep from going bankrupt. Games might be the only time we get to go out a big winner, whether it's making our way to the head of the class by answering questions or being the first to deduce that it was Mrs. Peacock in the study with a candlestick.

Proprietary board games date back to the eighteenth century, but the Big Kahuna is and has been Monopoly, the best-selling copyrighted game in the world.

For most of us, playing Monopoly was the first time in our lives that we had to make change for a ten (or thousand) dollar bill, borrow money from the bank, or deal with a landlord who wants his money now.

Monopoly went on the market in 1935, and since then Parker Brothers estimates more than 3 billion little wood (and later plastic) houses have been constructed in the 105 square inches of real estate on the famous board. More

than 250 million people have played the 100 million sets sold. The game is licensed in more than thirty countries and has been translated into twenty-three languages. It has spawned its own diseases ("Monopoly knees," from sitting cross-legged through an afternoon—or two) and has been translated into Braille.

Each set contains more than $15,000 in play money, and Parker Brothers prints more currency than the U.S. Treasury Department each year. The street names are from Atlantic City, New Jersey. In the English version, however, the setting is London, and Boardwalk and Park Place are Mayfair and Park Lane. It's called Monopol in Scandinavia, Monopoli in Italy, Rue de la

Paix in France. The currency is in Argentinian pesos, Belgian francs, Brazil's cruzeiros, El Salvador's colons, Greek drachmas, and Japanese yen.

The game is credited to Charles Darrow, who first offered it to Parker Brothers in 1934. The company rejected it, with one executive listing five fundamental playing errors. But after Darrow started selling copies on his own, Parker Brothers recanted and bought the rights. It wound up making Darrow a millionaire who traveled the globe collecting exotic orchids. Parker Brothers originally saw it as an adult game that would peak within a few years and was too "complicated" for kids. (Little did they know.)

Monopoly hasn't been without its controversies. In 1973, Ralph Anspach, a California-based economics professor, came up with a game called Anti-Monopoly, which sold well until Parker Brothers won a court action that stopped its sale. The ruling allowed forty thousand copies of Anti-Monopoly to be buried in a Minnesota landfill. Anspach later won a reversal in a higher court, in part because he proved Monopoly had actually evolved from an early-twentieth-century parlor game, The Landlord's Game, patented in 1904 by Elizabeth Magie, and that Darrow had made only a few changes.

In *The Monopoly Companion,* the company admits it's difficult to accept Darrow's explanation of how he created the game. Interestingly, Parker Brothers founder George Parker passed on The Landlord's Game when it was offered to him in 1924. Darrow himself apparently encountered another game called Finance, in which, as author Philip Orbanes writes, "you'll clearly see the footprint of Monopoly." Darrow didn't even change the names of the streets, including even the misspelling of Marven Gardens that remains Marvin Gardens today.

Whatever its origins, Monopoly was a godsend for a company struggling during the Depression, and the company didn't take any chances—it purchased the patents for both The Landlord's Game and Finance. The company still enforces its patents—in 1991, Parker Brothers filed trademark infringement suits against the manufacturer and retailers of a game called "Cityopoly."

If the game is played according to the manufacturer's rules, the average playing time usually isn't more than two hours. But Monopoly enthusiasts hardly are content with just playing the game—they seem to insist, for whatever reasons, on turning the game into something bigger (or in some cases, smaller), longer, and more dramatic. There are records for playing underground, in a bathtub, on a balance beam, upside down, underwater, on the back of a fire truck, and for the smallest game.

The longest game between two players, eighty hours, took place in 1971 in Danville, California. The year before, the longest Monopoly game played on an elevator was completed when a group of University of Kansas freshmen played fifty consecutive hours, while the elevator passed 7,212 floors. Six teens played fifty consecutive hours in a tree house in Louisville, Kentucky, in 1966.

The largest Monopoly game took place in April 1967 at Juniata College in Huntingdon, Pennsylvania. The playing board itself was larger than a city block, using campus streets and sidewalks. The dice were large foam-rubber cubes cast from a third-floor fire escape. Players were informed of one another's moves by messengers on bicycles equipped with walkie-talkies. At the other extreme, the smallest board is one inch square.

In 1961, University of Pennsylvania students in the midst of a marathon 160-hour game ran the bank out of money. They wired Parker Brothers for more cash, and the company sent $1 million in Monopoly money, delivered in a Brink's armored car under armed guard.

The game has had its effect on the real-life Atlantic City, too. In 1972, after a suggestion that the city needed a new image and a proposal considered changing the names of Baltic and Mediterranean avenues, residents and game lovers greeted the idea with a fire storm of anger and protest. The resolution was killed.

Parker Brothers is one of the oldest existing American toy companies. It was started in 1883 by sixteen-year-old George S. Parker, who took $40 of his savings to publish and market Banking, a game he invented. The company has published more than twelve hundred games in the years since. Parker Brothers was a family-owned company until 1968, when it became part of General Mills, where it stayed until 1985, when Kenner Products took over.

By 1888, after George had encouraged his sibling Charles to join him, Parker Brothers had twenty-nine games in its catalog, including The Railroad Game and Innocence Abroad, the latter a takeoff on the popular Mark Twain book of the same title. They also published The Game of American History, Presidential Game, Proverbs, Story of the Bible, The Game of Travel, and board-game versions of golf, bowling, and baseball.

The company learned to capitalize on current events during the Spanish-American War, introducing Hold the Fort, War in Cuba, The Siege of Havana, and Battle of Manila. In the early twentieth century it introduced three card games: Pit, an alternative to bridge; Flinch, which had a variety of games in its deck; and Rook; and all are still extant today. Touring, another Parker Broth-

THE GOAL OF CLUE WAS—AND STILL IS—TO GUESS THE IDENTITY OF A KILLER IN MR. BODDY'S MANSION, USING THE POWERS OF DEDUCTION. PLAYERS ELIMINATED SUSPECTS, MURDER WEAPONS, AND ROOMS ALONG THE WAY ON THEIR SCORECARDS.

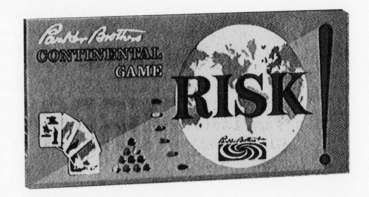

ers card game that had been introduced earlier, enjoyed a good run during the fifties, when the U.S. interstate system of highways was being built. The company also helped popularize jigsaw puzzles by cutting the pieces into recognizable shapes like lobsters, snowflakes, bull's heads, and stars.

Parker Brothers introduced three of its most successful board games in the fifties—Clue, Risk, and Careers. Risk was brought to the United States in 1959 through an association of Parker Brothers with the Miro Company in Paris to produce and manufacture each other's games in their respective countries. Clue was the product of a similar licensing and manufacturing arrangement, this one with Waddington Games Ltd. of Leeds, England.

Risk was a strategy game. The board showed the world—kind of—and as the rules state, "you battle to conquer the world." Players gained that world dominance by scheming "to eliminate your opponents by occupying every territory on the board." Plays are taken in three steps: getting and placing armies, attacking, and fortifying your position.

Possibilities seemed endless in Careers, where you could jump over a mountain, buy a yacht, find uranium, enter politics, go to the moon (a wild notion in 1956, remember), or prospect for gold. Players chose their own success formula—fame, happiness, or fortune—and spent the rest of the time rounding the board trying (usually in vain) to obtain it. Careers was advertised for ages eight to eighty.

MILTON BRADLEY MADE GAMES FOR THE WHOLE FAMILY.

In Sorry, players pursued each other around the board, with the object to get all their pawns home before anyone else by drawing special numbered cards. Going to Jerusalem was a journey to the Holy Land with the twelve apostles and a deck of cards—"an ideal way to learn Scriptural verses," Parker advertised.

Dig was another Parker game. When a card was turned, at the command "dig," players would take their magic picks and "dig" out letters to form words of subjects named on the card in front of them. Winners earned "shares" that could be traded for gold bars.

In 1962, Parker Brothers introduced Mille Bornes, a fast-moving French card game. The game (pronounced "meal born") was named after the cement road markers in France, and means "a thousand milestones." By drawing cards, the object was to travel a thousand miles along an unfamiliar route, dodging opponents' obstacles (flat tires, accidents) and preventing them from completing the same trip.

Another familiar toy company, Milton Bradley, is the oldest game and puzzle maker in existence. It was started by Milton Bradley, a lithographer who came up with a game called The Checkered Game of Life in 1860. The success of the game kept him in business, as he made modern versions of chess, checkers, backgammon, and tiddledywinks and created new games as the years went on. The company became the largest seller of jigsaw puzzles and now uses laser technology to cut the pieces. (Bradley also invented the single-handled paper trimmer in 1881, and was involved in the early kindergarten movement in the United States.)

The company introduced The Game of Life, an up-to-date version of The Checkered Game of Life, in celebration of its hundredth birthday in 1960. The goal in the original game was simply to achieve Happy Old Age by clean living and avoiding Ruin, and had the spiritual feeling to match. The new version was more materialistic; it gave each player a chance to become a millionaire, skirting the spiritual issue entirely. Let's get rich instead.

The Game of Life also updated the original by adding a three-dimensional element to the board, with bridges and lanes that went up and down and around the board. The game was perfectly designed to emulate the postwar era's values: The monetary stakes were higher than in Monopoly, and as any good baby-boomer family should be, players were rewarded for the number of children they could squeeze onto their little pastel-colored plastic automobiles. "If you get more than four children, just crowd them in as you do in real life!" advised the rules sagely.

The game was enhanced by the use of a spinner (a miniature precursor to "Wheel of Fortune") and a colorful numbers board so you could gamble your salary away on other players' turns. You could win huge amounts of money by doing nothing more than landing on the right squares. Compared to Monopoly's puny $15,000—and remember, that was a lot of money in those days—The Game of Life's bank totaled more than $13 million. There was plenty of money to be made.

Chutes and Ladders has seen enduring popularity since its mass-produced introduction in 1943. The game came to America from England with the early settlers. The object was to get from one side of the board to the other. Players could either get a boost from landing on a ladder or slide backwards by landing on a chute. Since it took only a rudimentary knowledge of numbers and no reading ability, the game was perfect for kids aged four to ten.

Candy Land was introduced six years later, created by Eleanor Abbott of San Diego, California, during her recuperation from polio. The game eliminates reading and counting by basing play on matching colors and objects. Players advance along a rainbow path using gingerbread men as playing pieces. Milton Bradley estimates that more than 100 million people have traversed the Peppermint Stick Forest, the Gingerbread Plum Tree, and Gum Drop Mountain on the 20 million sets sold since then.

The Game of the States gave players the opportunity to move trucks from state to state buying and selling products.

Go to the Head of the Class was introduced by the company in 1938. Invented by two New York department store employees, the game allowed players to answer questions and move from desk to desk in the mock-classroom layout. The first to graduate is the winner. By 1982 it was in its twenty-third edition.

Cadaco-Ellis has also been popular—and prolific—with its board games. Tripoley, a board game that combined Michigan rummy, hearts, and poker, and came complete with a green felt casino-style tablecloth, had been produced by the company since the thirties. But the game hit its stride in the fifties and sixties. The game remains popular because there are several ways to win during each hand, which keeps everyone interested. Over the years it has developed offshoots like Three-Dimensional Tripoley, and now comes in different editions.

Cadaco also produced a three-dimensional game for preschoolers called The Undersea World Game, in which plastic fish were the playing pieces and each player tried to get the most fish for his aquarium. Touch and Go was a two-person game that took some skill to learn, as players picked up little steel balls with their magic wands and tried to slide the magnetized balls over the target area.

The Mother Goose Game was a trip down Nursery Rhyme Lane with all the fairy-tale favorites in attendance. The Ten Commandments Bible Game had players travel around a board that included the River Jordan, Mt. Sinai, and the Sea of Galilee, meeting Philistines, lepers, Roman centurions, and nomads, picking up Ten Commandment cards along the way. Noah's Ark was the preschoolers' version, in which the object was to fill the boat with stand-up animals. Sharpshooter, a target game, came with a rubber-band pistol to hit grizzlies, rhinos, and moose; when they were killed, they turned instantly into rugs. Decisions, Decisions was a marbles game that demanded quick thinking to keep from losing them.

In Dead Pan, players dropped a marble into a pan, let it fall at random, and added up the score. World-Wide Geography pitted players against time across oceans, continents, seas, rivers, and islands around the globe. In Pirate Raid, players searched for treasure. Thirteen was based on the multiplication tables. Spell-It used a colorful wheel device and board to teach spelling and arithmetic. Space Pilot, an action game with a spinner that was a spaceship, planet pegs, and a cardboard "interplanetary flying field," took you to unknown planets.

For small-fry fishermen, Hookey used magnets instead of live bait to lure the big ones. Little Black Sambo, based on the children's story, followed footsteps through the jungle, trying to elude tigers along the way. (The game's popularity paled with the onset of civil rights consciousness.) Travel With Woody Woodpecker featured that wascal woodpecker, who was forever forcing looney changes in direction as you flew around the world.

One of the most familiar games of the past few decades is the ubiquitous Carrom board, a two-sided square wooden board with corner pockets. The board was designed to accommodate a number of different games according to the players' whims. One side had a standard checkerboard and often backgammon, the other had a crokinole layout. It came with a variable number of playing pieces, including little rings and miniature bowling pins, to play 80 to 100 games. Many were variations of basics like ring carrom, pocket billiards, crokinole, backgammon, checkers, chess, and bowling variations. Most of the games involved moving the rings around, either with a flick of the finger or with cue sticks.

The Carrom game was actually made by two different companies after 1960, when a group of executives broke from the parent company, Carrom Industries, and went exclusively into the game business with a similar board they called Carom. That offshoot, Merdel Manufacturing Co., finally bought the Carrom name in 1976 and continues to sell the games today, along with air hockey, shuffleboard, pool tables, and Bowl-A-Mania.

Gusher, a prewar game based on the oil business, was reintroduced by Carrom Industries in the fifties. Fox Hunt, a game that used a spinning top ricocheting through a maze and knocking down pins, is now manufactured as Skittles, and has been called Racketeer. Carrom also manufactured Arkitoy, a wood building set, and Kikit, an early ancestor of contemporary Foos-Ball. Nok-Hockey, an action game with little hockey sticks, is still made today.

Herb Schaper, a Minneapolis mailman who whittled fishing lures while walking his route, found that one in the shape of a flea caught children's eyes. In 1948, with $75 in investment capital and a game called Cootie, he started Schaper Toys.

Schaper eventually developed a line of forty toys and games. Stadium Checkers was a plastic variation on regular checkers. The object was to move your marbles into the middle of a tiered plastic stadium by moving the tiers back and forth and letting the marbles roll down. Skunk used special skunk dice and colored chips, and players tried to build a score of 100

THE VERSATILE CARROM BOARD, ON WHICH A HUNDRED GAMES CAN BE PLAYED, HASN'T CHANGED DESIGN SINCE ITS INTRODUCTION AT THE TURN OF THE CENTURY.

COOTIE WAS A PLASTIC INSECT ASSEMBLED PIECE BY PIECE WITH A ROLL OF THE DICE. IT TAUGHT AN EARLY LESSON ABOUT THE RISKS OF A DICE GAME.

YAHTZEE USED DICE TO PLAY POKER. FIVE DICE WERE ROLLED THREE TIMES EACH TURN AS PLAYERS TRIED TO COME UP WITH COMBINATIONS LIKE THREE OF A KIND, FOUR OF A KIND, FULL HOUSE (THREE OF ONE DICE AND TWO OF ANOTHER), STRAIGHT (ALL DICE IN ORDER SEQUENTIALLY), AND ALL FIVE DICE THE SAME, THE COVETED YAHTZEE. IT SOUNDED SIMPLE, BUT THE POSSIBILITIES WERE ENDLESS, AND STRATEGY— INCLUDING THE UBIQUITOUS BLUFF—WAS IMPORTANT.

points or more and avoid being "skunked." Mill was a variation on a European game known as Morelles or Muhle.

Another Schaper game, Pig in the Garden, featured miniature vegetables planted in a garden on the board. A bug rolled down a plastic track in Tumble Bug. Twizzle was another marble game. In King of the Hill players used a "tilt move" selector to advance up and down a hill. Guess 'n Bee was an early predecessor of Wheel of Fortune; contestants guessed a preset word before getting stung by the bee.

A wealthy Canadian couple invented The Yacht Game to play when friends came aboard their yacht. They took it to Edwin S. Lowe, a man who had sold bingo

games in the twenties, to make samples as gifts for friends. Lowe liked the game and bought it from the couple outright in exchange for a few copies of the game, changed the name to Yahtzee, and introduced it in the early fifties. A mixture of dice and poker, it was advertised with "the fun game that makes thinking…fun" written on the bald, furrowed brow of a smiling eggheaded fellow. Other Lowe games included Scribbage, Real Bingo, Bet-A-Million, Renaissance Chessmen, and Chess Tutor.

Selchow and Righter, which created Parcheesi in 1867, made its fortune with Scrabble, the world-famous word game with 3.2 billion possible seven-

letter combinations. The game has been translated over the years into French, German, Italian, Russian, Spanish, and Hebrew, and 2 million sets are sold every year. The game's social interaction is still popular enough that more than a hundred Scrabble clubs meet regularly in the United States to play tournaments.

Television game shows have their roots in radio game shows, which in turn were rooted in parlor and card games. Programs like "Uncle Jim's Question Bee" and "Professor Quiz," which debuted in the thirties, set the standard for quiz shows: answer questions, and if you answer right, you win money. The first big give-

away—a thousand dollars—came on "Pot O' Gold" in 1939, a program also credited with being the first to require players to choose whether they wanted to go ahead and risk everything at each plateau.

In 1940, Ralph Edwards began "Truth or Consequences," a silly quiz show which penalized you for not answering (or answering too late) by making you perform some ridiculous

task, like putting a pillowcase on with boxing gloves. By 1948, a pre–Miss America host Bert Parks emceed "Stop the Music," a radio program that offered contestants a chance to win not money but stoves, refrigerators, and washing machines by naming song titles before their opponents—a prototype for the television-era "Name That Tune."

But the postwar generation wasn't weaned on radio; it was raised on television.

The first TV game show was "Cash and Carry," which debuted in 1946 with host Dennis James on a set that was a country grocery store stocked with

sponsor Libby's canned goods. Soon America was crazy about boob tube game shows. "Winner Take All" in 1948 introduced the contestant who continued playing until he or she lost, and for the first time used a buzzer to help create drama. "What's My Line" was one of the early popular games, with celebrities guessing people's occupations and the identity of a "mystery guest." Americans played "Beat the Clock" with Bud Collyer, "Truth or Consequences" with Jack Bailey and Bob Barker, "Tic Tac Dough" and "Twenty One" with Jack Barry, "Let's Make a Deal" with Monty Hall, "Concentration" with Hugh Downs, and "Jeopardy" with Art Fleming.

Mike Stokey introduced the charades parlor game to television with "Pantomime Quiz" in 1947. Besides using actors and comedians to act out pithy sayings and quotes, Stokey speeded up the action for the benefit of TV's short attention span. Other classic games introduced to television in the fifties included "Tic-Tac-Toe," "Hangman" (later revived as "Wheel of Fortune"), "Blackjack," "20 Questions," and "High Low."

It didn't take long for producers and toy makers to figure out that most of the games could be played in home editions, and that people loved to pretend to be Allen Ludden while running their own living-room version of "Password."

The Concentration home game was a classic television-turned-home game. The game itself was similar to Memory or Husker Du: you exposed the puzzle by remembering where prizes were and matching them up, winning the prizes if you could guess the puzzle. And in the home version, you didn't have to decide how you were going to get the rolltop desk or the jukebox back to your home—you won them only figuratively. The puzzles were placed on a roller, about forty games per issue, and Concentration added new editions to keep up with the demand for more puzzles—it didn't take long to memorize all the phrases on one roll.

On the home version of "The $64,000 Question," which was popular on the screen until scandals racked the industry in the late fifties, contestants answered the $8,000, $16,000, and $32,000 questions before finally taking on the big one. Presumably, unlike its television counterpart, the home game wasn't rigged. Other board games based on TV programs included Break the Bank, Dollar a Second, Tic Tac Dough, and The Match Game. You could play along with Jan Murray's Treasure Hunt, a game in which prizes were hidden in little chests carried around by Marion Stafford, the "Pirate Girl," an early version of Vanna White. Later Murray hosted the word game "Charge Account."

You didn't have to have a game show to have a home version. For some, simply being on TV was enough. Television tie-ins were seen as keys to selling toys by manufacturers, who trumpeted the number of people who would see the ads on the screen.

171

## THE TOY BOOK

"Ten million Pinky Lee fans will want this game," boasted an ad for Pinky Lee and the Runaway Frankfurters, in which players pursued hot dogs and frankfurter stands around a colorful board. Ideal's Stump the Stars, a celebrity charades game aired Mondays on CBS, was tied in with Chex cereals.

The I'm George Gobel Game was based on Lonesome George's laid-back comedy and variety program; in Adventures of Lassie, you relived the collie's television experiences by trying to be the first to reach the famous pooch's doghouse (really!); and in You'll Never Get Rich, you matched wits with Sgt. Bilko, the fast-talking television platoon leader played by Phil Silvers. Players tripped through Fantasyland, Tomorrowland, Frontierland, and Adventureland in the Electric Disneyland Tours board game. Each land also had its own game versions. In The Lone Ranger and the Silver Bullets, you accumulated silver shells just like the mysterious masked man's.

No show was exempt. Lowell designed games around private-eye series like "Peter Gunn," "77 Sunset Strip," and "Surfside 6," and another on the Three Stooges. The long-running detective show

## GAMES PEOPLE PLAY

IN 1962, "THE BEVERLY HILL-
BILLIES" WAS THE HIGHEST-
RATED TV SHOW, SO IT WAS NO
SURPRISE THAT THE NEXT YEAR
IT WOULD BE TRANSFERRED
ONTO A GAME BOARD.

"Dragnet" had its own board game, where you could be Joe Friday gathering evidence, interrogating suspects, and hanging out with criminals—just like Jack Webb. The board was a city with streets and buildings where you could find, apprehend, and bring in your man.

Barnabas Collins's vampirish grin leered out from Milton Bradley's Dark Shadows game, based on the popular late-sixties horrific soap opera (which was stylishly reprised in 1991). "The Beverly Hillbillies," the campy hicks-go-to-Hollywood sitcom, was briefly immortalized in its own board game, manu-

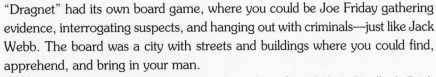

factured by Standard Toykraft. Just in case you didn't get the point, the company emblazoned the box with a huge eye, the logo for the "Hillbillies" network. Hey, you! the logo screamed out at customers, this is on TV, so you should own it!

Both "Dr. Kildare" and "Ben Casey" debuted in 1961, and you could play along with hunk Richard Chamberlain in the Dr. Kildare Medical Game for the Young, or put together a picture puzzle of antihero Vince Edwards placing the stethoscope on some miraculously cured child. It even included an autographed picture of Vince on the box. Dr. Kildare and Ben Casey also got their faces cut up into their own jigsaw puzzles, all made by Milton Bradley.

The game called Why was a family mystery much like Clue that was popularized by the success of "Alfred Hitchcock Presents," a program known as much for the famous director's introductions as for its scary stories. "Password," in which one person tried to get a partner to say a word by using synonyms, was perfect for the home market, with new passbooks regularly added to meet demand.

One unusual gameshow tie-in reversed the relationship of home games modeled after TV programs. Milton Bradley's "Shenanigans" TV program was a life-size version of the home game's carnival arcade-style playing board. Players on the television program made

their way through each contest of skill and memory, just like the players at home.

Although it wasn't a game show per se, perhaps the ultimate television-game link for kids was "Winky Dink and You," an early TV program hosted by Jack Barry. Barry allowed himself to be the straight man for Winky, a glowing electronic gremlin with big ears. But the magic of "Winky Dink" was that you got involved at home.

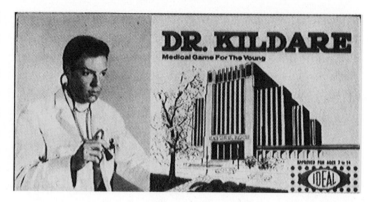

"You can't be part of the program without the magic window," Barry would remind viewers every few minutes. Kids placed the magic window, purchased for only 50 cents, on the screen, where it stuck because of static electricity. They used black, red, yellow, and green "magic crayons" to help Winky cross bridges or create mayhem, and later erased it with the magic cloth.

Of course, those who didn't have the magic windows would still see Winky walk across the invisible bridge, and many parents gave up the 50 cents rather than have their kids use regular Crayolas directly on the screen, creating their own bridges.

Movie tie-ins worked, too. When Walt Disney released the film *20,000 Leagues Under the Sea* during the 1954 Christmas season, merchandise included the 20,000 Leagues Under the Sea Electric Quiz Game: Playway to Knowledge for All Ages. Besides having a long name, the game gave

players the chance to match up numbers with descriptions by using metal-tipped cords. The correct answers lit up—it just couldn't be used underwater.

Games tied in with other media besides television included the Camp Grenada Game, based on the song "Hello Muddah Hello Fadduh! (A Letter

PLAYERS COULD ALMOST HEAR ALFRED HITCHCOCK INTONING "GOOD EVENING" AS THEY UNRAVELED A MYSTERIOUS DEATH IN THE MILTON BRADLEY BOARD GAME WHY. THE GAME'S PLAYING PIECES WERE CLEVER SPOOFS OF FAMILIAR DETECTIVES: SHY-LOCK BONES, DICK CRAZY, CHARLIE CLAM, AND SERGEANT MONDAY.

## GAMES PEOPLE PLAY

from Camp)," a hit for Allan Sherman in 1963. The idea, like that of the song (sample lyric: "I went hiking with Joe Spivey, he developed poison ivy, you remember Leonard Skinner, he got ptomaine poisoning last night after dinner"), was to get out of camp.

Snoopy and the Red Baron was patterned on the Peanuts cartoon strip drawn by Charles Schulz and included the inevitable air combat with the World War I flying ace. Peanuts was so popular toward the late sixties that dozens of licensing agreements allowed Peanuts-related toys (stuffed animals, books, plastic squeeze toys, and even sheets and bedspreads, sweatshirts, and other clothing), including other Peanuts games, like Milton Bradley's Good Ol' Charlie Brown, to proliferate.

In 1964, the year when sociologist Marshall McLuhan made his famous remark "The medium is the message," Milton Bradley even made a promotional tie-in to a media event that wasn't part of the mass media: the New York

175

World's Fair. The company was the exclusive game and puzzlemaker for the fair, which opened in 1964 and ran through the next year. Milton Bradley's World's Fair line, which retailed from 29 cents to $2, included a Panorama Game, Children's and Adult's Boxed Puzzle Assortments, World on the String, and the World's Fair Game.

With the classic board games well established, manufacturers in the sixties began experimenting with novel ways to expand the game market. One way was to aim games at specific markets, instead of creating family games. Most games are designed for both boys and girls, but in the sixties some games were aimed at one sex.

Mattel's Sonar Sub-Hunt, a toy for battle-hungry boys, used a battery-powered "sonar scope" to track enemy submarines. The players watched the action through periscopes and triggered mines and depth charges to sink each other's subs. When a hit was scored, the sonar game board lit up with the explosion.

Mattel also took advantage of the company's phenomenal success with Barbie dolls, and created the Barbie's Keys to Fame game for girls. The object of the game was to win all the cards and the right key to a great Barbie career: movie star, ballerina, stewardess, fashion designer, nurse, mother, teacher, or astronaut (pretty progressive for 1964—long before America's first woman astronaut, Sally Ride, flew into space). "This game's got everything," Mattel proudly proclaimed, "…including the magic name of BARBIE!"

For boys, Milton Bradley had Pow!, a cannon game; for girls there was Wow!, designed around a pillow fight. In the mid-sixties, just as the women's movement was starting to form, the company treated young girls to the first edition of Mystery Date, one of the more bizarre fantasy games of the decade. The television ads were hilarious, with girls excitedly playing the game to find out who they'd be asked out by: "Will he be a dream [the hidden card showed a suave, collegiate stud] or a dud [awww, he's a slobby beach bum]?" To find out, girls lifted the door at the center of the playing board to view the "date" that had secretly been inserted at the start.

Some games were aimed at younger players, including Barrel of Monkeys by Lakeside. The object of the game, a distant cousin to Pick-

## GAMES PEOPLE PLAY

Up-Sticks, was to use extended arms of the plastic, brightly colored monkeys to pick up all twelve chimps. If you were shaky, the monkeys would all tumble down and you'd have to start from scratch.

But the gold mine for sixties games lay in a host of gimmicks that added new twists to old ideas.

The ultimate gimmick game was Ideal's 1963 winner, Mouse Trap Game. The game was played on a folding playing board, but with a number of plastic parts pressed in place to make a three-dimensional playing area of mind-boggling complexity. The game was an immediate smash—Ideal sold more than 1.2 million copies of Mouse Trap the first year.

The company didn't waste any time coming up with other gadget-laden games by the next Christmas season. The Crazy Clock Game was a slight variation on Mouse Trap, with suspiciously similar pieces connecting an elaborate contraption that added zaniness to the basic board game. Mystic Skull was "the Game of Voodoo," a board game embellished with a "mysterious moving skull" and the board's centerpiece, a cooking pot for human sacrifices. In 1965, Ideal added Hands Down, a quick-action game that featured "the colorful exciting Slam-O-Matic!" The object was to draw numbered cards and beat your opponents by being the first to slap your hands down on the Slam-O-Matic centerpiece, shaped like four plastic hands.

Some action games didn't have a board at all. Milton Bradley's Time Bomb gave a more dangerous edge to the toy called Hot Potato, a spud with a windup timer; the object was to toss it back and forth and not be stuck holding it when the timer ran out. Time Bomb worked the same way, except it was shaped like a round bomb complete with a "fuse" you wound up for the timer. It let you know time ran out with a loud "bang."

The supernatural was a popular preoccupation in the late sixties, with such media stars as Kreskin making his way into gamedom with his Amazing Kreskin ESP game. The grandfather of them all was the Ouija board, but there was plenty of competition from such games as The Mystery Zodiac Game, The Green Ghost Game (with a centerpiece that glowed in the dark), Ka-Bala (less a game than a fortune-telling toy, again with a glow-in-the-dark centerpiece), and Which Witch.

Action was the key word with other games. And the ultimate action game was Rock 'Em Sock 'Em Robots. The toy, created by Marx, was a miniature boxing ring with red and blue robots glaring at each other, which were connected to hand controls outside the ring. The players began fighting with the robots, swinging away until a sock to the jaw popped the loser's head up. "You knocked his block off!" the TV commercials exclaimed excitedly. Ideal resurrected the Robots in the late eighties with only slight updates: a high-tech color scheme and one robot's vaguely "Robocop"–like head.

Bash! was a game of skill that involved hammering a plastic disc out of a stack serving as the "body" of a comical character. You lost if you knocked over the character. The object of Hoop-La was to snag as many tiny hoops as possible, using a clown riding a unicycle around the game's wire perimeter. If the clown fell, you lost. Kerplunk was a game of second-guessing; the clear plastic cylinder had a midsection into which you stuck a number of toothpicks, then you poured marbles in the top. The object was to pull out toothpicks without the marbles crashing down.

Operation, a Milton Bradley game that's still on the shelves, required the removal of mock-anatomical parts from a cardboard patient splayed out on an operating table. The trick was to operate with care, because you dragged out the "funny bone," for instance, with a pair of tweezers hooked up by wires to a battery-run buzzer. If the "doctor" slipped and touched the sides of the incision, the patient's nose lit up and the loud buzzer went off, scaring the player enough to drop the bone instead of extracting it.

One manufacturer, Kohner Bros., even managed to add action features to basic, roll-the-dice board games. The object of games such as Trouble and Headache was simple: You rolled dice to get around the board as quickly as possible, with as few penalties as possible. The novelty of these two, however, was that instead of a regular roll of the dice, players turned to a clear plastic dome at the center of the game board, which contained the dice. You pushed the dome down, and let go—a metal spring underneath "popped" and jumbled the dice within the dome. Hence the catchy name for the device, "Pop-O-Matic." Kohner also created a non–Pop-O-Matic game, Hat's Off, where players tried to catapult all their plastic cone-shaped hats into their respective slots in the game board first.

The king of sixties game fads, though, didn't have playing pieces at all: The players themselves were the pieces, and Twister brought a new meaning

THE GOAL OF TWISTER WAS TO OUTLAST OPPONENTS BY STRETCHING AND ENTWINING YOUR BODY LIKE A HUMAN PRETZEL AROUND A LARGE VINYL SHEET EMBLAZONED WITH MULTICOLORED CIRCLES, WITHOUT FALLING DOWN. WITH MORE THAN TWO PLAYERS, THE VINYL SHEET GOT SO CROWDED THAT THE RESULTS WERE OFTEN HILARIOUS, AND SOMETIMES DOWNRIGHT LEWD.

OTHER COMPANIES STUDIED MILTON BRADLEY'S SUCCESS WITH THE TEEN-ORIENTED TWISTER, AND CAME UP WITH GOOFIER VARIATIONS ON THE THEME. PARKER BROTHERS CREATED FUNNY BONES, A "SOCIAL INTERACTION" GAME THAT HAD CARDS WITH NURSERY RHYME COMMANDS LIKE "HEAD BONE CONNECTED TO THE ELBOW BONE," OR "BACK BONE CONNECTED TO THE HAND BONE." PLAYERS DID WHAT THE CARDS SAID, OFTEN RESULTING IN COMICAL POSES.

to the phrase "contact sports." The game, not surprisingly, was a huge hit on college campuses. In fact, it still is. In 1987, a record-breaking 4,160 contestants tied themselves up in knots playing a Twister marathon at the University of Massachusetts in Amherst.

Twister was the subject of a huge publicity campaign when it was introduced in 1966. After Johnny Carson and Eva Gabor hooked themselves together in front of millions of viewers on the "Tonight" show in May of that year, the rush was on to buy the game. Considering the simplicity of its design (the vinyl sheet was the greatest expense of the package), Twister has been a profit-making dream for Milton Bradley.

By the end of the heady sixties, both traditional board games and the newer fad games had had their day. One of the popular items in 1968 was an unassuming Parker Brothers creation, Instant Insanity. The game was simply four plastic cubes with different-colored sides. The object of the puzzle was to stack the four cubes so each side of the stack had four different colors showing. Instant Insanity established a sales record for its first year by selling 7 million units. The cube was often promoted in ads and commercials by the hapless, befuddled Pat Paulsen, then star of "The Smothers Brothers Comedy Hour."

Instant Insanity was resurrected in a variation during the seventies as the Rubik's Cube. Other puzzles followed in the wake of Instant Insanity, including Drive Ya Nuts, a layout of plastic nuts that had to be rearranged so every touching side had matching numbers. Parker Brothers in 1969 followed Instant Insanity with Soma, a cube assembled out of seven seemingly simple but maddeningly complex pieces.

If the Vietnam War made war toys unpopular, it didn't seem to affect war-oriented games much. Two popular board games of the late sixties were Stratego, a chesslike game of battle strategy, and Battleship, a game

where you tried to outsmart your opponents by trying to guess—and blow up—the locations of their battleships. With baby boomers getting older every year, manufacturers also found ways to appeal to older game players. More intellectual, "bookshelf" games were created,

BEFORE RUBIK'S CUBE, THERE WAS INSTANT INSANITY, A COLOR-CODED PUZZLE WHICH PAT PAULSEN NEVER SEEMED TO CONQUER.

LATER IN THE SIXTIES, COMPANIES BEGAN CREATING GAMES LIKE STRATEGO FOR OLDER, MORE SOPHISTICATED PLAYERS.

including complex games of strategy often set to historical battles, and other games based on economics or business.

As professional sports grew in prominence—mostly because of television—so did the desire for board games that approximated the feel of the sports themselves. The entire nation, it seemed, was watching when New York Yankee pitcher Don Larsen pitched the first (and only) perfect game during the World Series in 1956. The National Football League came into its own after the 1958 championship game between the Baltimore Colts

and the New York Giants that ended with Alan Ameche's famous trap run touchdown in sudden-death overtime. Sports was big time, and toy makers responded with innovations.

Cadaco was founded as Cadaco-Ellis in 1935. The first game the company produced was Varsity Football, which is still in the company's line today as All-American Football. By the sixties, when the company was sold to Rapid Mounting and Finishing and moved to

Chicago, the company was producing popular games like Bas-Ket, Pro Foto-Football, and All-Star Baseball, most of which were first marketed in the forties and fifties.

Bas-Ket, now NBA Bas-Ket, was a three-dimensional basketball game with a celluloid Ping-Pong--sized ball. It rolled around the irregular playing surface, landing in one of twelve shooting holes. Players then used mechanical steel levers to shoot the ball at cardboard backboards. The original cloth nets later were replaced with plastic. The action was fast, and you had to learn the secrets of each shooting lever, just as real players had to learn the idiosyncrasies of the parquet floor in Boston Garden, because despite being made on the assembly line, no two shooters were ever quite the same. Today's NBA Bas-Ket changed the long shot into a three-pointer.

The Gotham Pressed Steel Corporation came up with its own version. The Pass 'N Shoot Basketball Game allowed players to shoot, pass, or defend against shots, but otherwise, the game was similar to Bas-Ket.

Other games in the Bas-Ket mold included Match Point Tennis, where players could control their serves and return the ball from any of the ten holes on the playing surface, and All Star Hockey, where shots were taken with the same mechanical levers as Bas-Ket and each player protected the net with a realistic goalie on the cardboard rink. Cadaco also offered the Fun 'n Games Table Set, a fiberboard game table that came with two stools. The plastic-covered table could be folded up—which made it perfect for vacations or the beach or poolside—and had about fifteen game boards on it—enough for a hundred different contests.

Electric games were already popular, if somewhat primitive, in the late forties. In 1947 the Electric Game Co. of Holyoke, Massachusetts, offered Electric Football, Bowling, and Baseball, early, basic versions of electric boards, alongside more traditional skittle-type games such as Whiz Football, Bowling, and Baseball.

As the years went by, developers at Gotham and the Tudor Metal Products Corporation worked on making the games more realistic. The closer the board versions matched the excitement and intensity of professional sports events, the more popular they were, and it helped to update packages with the familiar athletic superstars of the day.

Most electric games of the period operated by making tiny plastic figures vibrate up and down a metal playing surface. They haven't really changed much—even today.

Electric football was the most obvious. As coach, you could set up your team at the line of scrimmage in any formation before pressing the button and watching the players scatter around while the field vibrated and the room buzzed like Dad's fancy new electric shaver. The pieces were sculpted to look like linemen, ends, offensive or defensive backs, and a spring-driven quarterback "threw" the ball. Many of the models had a kicker, also spring-driven, who tried to put field goals through the tiny uprights at either end of the field. A marker attached to the sidelines kept track of the line of scrimmage.

The simplest models were like sandlots in comparison with the more elaborate stadium fields, like Gotham's, which in 1961 came complete with a grandstand along one side of the field and a bleacher section behind each end zone. There were even pennants at the top of the grandstand for each NFL team of the time.

Nobody seemed to mind how noisy these electric games were—though later models had a pad placed around the players' mounting to deaden the buzz. Too often the players either fell down or changed direction. Who can forget the horror of watching your halfback eluding all pursuers down the sidelines for an uncontested touch—er, safety? A screw at one end of the field controlled how much the playing surface vibrated. Turn it down and the players moved in ultra-slow motion (just like the famous NFL films); turn it up and all twenty-two players would fall down. After a frustrating loss, it was always fun to turn it up and laugh as the little players gyrated spastically in all directions.

Electric baseball operated on the same principle, and companies began making all kinds of sports games in electric or electromagnetic models. The colorful metal and Masonite fields looked like real baseball stadiums, com-

CADACO-ELLIS'S ALL-STAR BASE-BALL GAME WAS DESIGNED BY A PRO, ETHAN ALLAN, WHO PLAYED WITH THE ST. LOUIS CARDINALS AND THE NEW YORK GIANTS.

BAS-KET SIMULATED REAL BAS-KETBALL ACTION IN MINIATURE.

plete with bleachers, advertising signs, and a big scoreboard in center field. In electric baseball, the painted players in the dugouts were always ready to pinch-hit or relieve the pitcher, and the fans in the stands constantly cheered.

Some models used a metal pitcher that threw a tiny magnetic ball to a wooden replica of a Louisville Slugger at the touch of a button. Wherever the ball landed determined the type of play—if it hit an infielder it was an out; if it cleared the bleachers and stuck to the blue sky, it was a homer, and you could pretend you were Roger Maris, Harmon Killebrew, or Mickey Mantle.

When the ball was in play, the excitement began. With the juice turned on, a runner similar to the football player headed for first base on a track that circled the infield.

By the sixties, the pitching device on many models had changed and wasn't operated electrically. The wooden bat became plastic, and was operated by a plastic spring; the game had become reduced to a miniature version of Wiffle ball, not baseball.

ELECTRIC BASEBALL GAMES GOT A LOT MORE COMPLICATED THAN THIS PLAIN 1947 BATTERY-OPERATED DIAMOND. IT DIDN'T EVEN COME WITH BLEACHERS OR PLAYERS LIKE LATER MODELS.

FOOTBALL, BASEBALL, AND HOCKEY LAYOUTS AND PLAYING FIGURES BECAME MORE REALISTIC AS THE YEARS WENT BY.

Not all sports games were electric-powered, nor were they all styled after basketball, baseball, or football. Hubley's Golferino celebrated that more civilized sport with a tabletop version of miniature golf. An outside knob and lever controlled "Mr. Golferino," and aimed his putter in the direction of the nine different holes—all fraught with the same obstacles you encountered down at the miniature golf course.

Hockey is one sport that's been popular in both mechanical and electric versions. Mechanical hockey games often were jostled as kids inevitably got carried away trying to twist their players to take shots. Later, electric air hockey became the rage of both amusement arcades and home versions, where two contestants faced off against each other and slapped around a light plastic "puck" floating on a cushion of air shot out of holes that dotted the playing field.

The more traditional electric hockey game had an automatic scoring device. Players twisted and turned and scooted up and down their designated areas, trying to block shots by the other team or initiating their own, and were operated manually with levers. As the years went by, the rink was lowered to keep the puck in play more easily. By 1970, the levers had been replaced by dials that made it easier to control players.

Tudor also made an electric Track Meet, Horse Race, and Harness Race, all three of which had a circular track and either runners, jockeys on horses, or jockeys in harnesses. A later Track and Field Meet included the discus throw, pole vault, and javelin as well as runners.

MANUFACTURERS EVEN FOUND WAYS TO MINIATURIZE GOLF FOR HOME PLAY. IN GOLFERINO, PLAYERS CONTROLLED A COMICAL GOLFER WITH LEVERS; THE ARNOLD PALMER TABLE GOLF GAME CAME WITH ACCESSORIES (A METAL FAIRWAY, FELT GREEN, CHANGEABLE HAZARDS) TO SIMULATE DIFFERENT HOLES, AND A MINIATURE MECHANICAL PUTTER FOR EACH PLAYER.

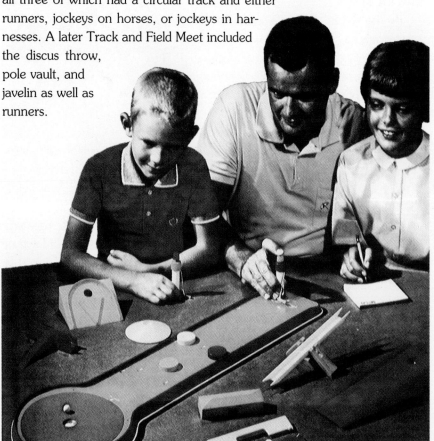

These electric games were the precursors of the computerized electronic games to come in the seventies and eighties. Throughout the sixties, the electronics industry refined its technology to make products smaller, faster, and smarter—think of the first hand-held calculators, and how much they cost. By the late seventies, tiny computers that had cost $400 a few years before could be purchased for under $100.

The same advances were applied to toys and eventually changed the entire toy industry, especially the home-game market, by switching its focus to hardware/software lines instead of hardy, perennial board games.

The first major electronic video game was Pong. The digital version of Ping-Pong (a family game many baby boomers knew through the rickety table-tennis sets their parents crammed into the basement family rooms alongside the bumper pool table) was first introduced to public arcades, restaurants, and bars through the same distributors that managed pinball machines and jukeboxes. But the Atari Corporation, a leader in the development of home computer games, created the first great toy fad of the seventies with its home version of Pong.

The game was relatively simple to play, and so it was deceptively engaging. The problem was that it was so easy to get caught up in playing Pong that you'd waste away hours trying to outmaneuver your opponents and rack up the highest scores. The Pong mechanism hooked up to your home television screen; when it was connected and turned on, the screen gave off a dull glow broken at both sides by small computer prompters that served as "paddles," which were controlled by tabletop knobs. The screen was split down the middle by an electronic "net" marking off the sides.

When the game commenced, an electronic blip bounced from side to side in an approximation of a Ping-Pong ball, using the sides of the screen to create unpredictable angular trajectories. The object of the game was to send the "ball" spinning (with a little practice, you could put English on it by timing the

185

paddle slash just right) past your opponent. The game was cleverly designed to hook you with the excitement of increased challenge: the longer you volleyed back and forth, the faster the ball bounced. With a pair of experienced players, the action was breathtaking, and the tense adrenaline flow overwhelming.

Home video games have developed ever since from the larger versions created for the arcade amusement industry: car and motorcycle racing, jet battles, Pac-Man, space attacks, and even the latest evolution in electronic sports games—video football, baseball, basketball, and newer sensations, such as Nintendo.

But the computer age marked the end of the era when the toy industry grew up with the baby boom generation. By the early seventies, the first kids born after World War II were out of college and already settling into their careers. The last of the kids born during the official duration of the boom were ten years old and consumed video games with a voracious passion. But they'd been raised with such a dazzling array of innovations in the world around them that their attention spans were short. Manufacturers had to scramble constantly to search for the Next Big Thing in the toy world, just to satisfy the new market's demands.

ATARI'S PONG SIMULATED PING-PONG ON YOUR HOME TV SCREEN—IT WAS THE FIRST WELL-KNOWN ELECTRONIC GAME.

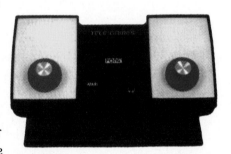

And because that new market was smaller than the one during the height of the boom, the toy fads of the seventies and eighties had to saturate the market completely to be as successful as even the passing fancies of ten years earlier. Many of the crazier fads of the past two decades—Pet Rocks, Rubik's Cube, Cabbage Patch Dolls—reached dizzying sales figures very quickly, but dropped out of sight almost as quickly (Cabbage Patch Dolls, the biggest craze of the early eighties, were so in demand that the manufacturer, Coleco, placed too much empha-

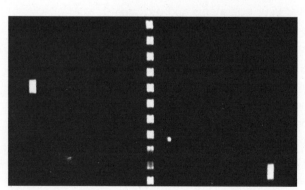

sis on the dolls in its line, and within a few years filed for bankruptcy protection).

The toys of the fifties and sixties resonate in a generation's hearts and minds not just because we grew up with them (though that's certainly part of the attraction), but because the entire world was bending over backwards to serve our slightest whims. The generation that couldn't be ignored was instead being pampered and courted by toy companies, as we were later pampered and courted by schools, businesses, car manufacturers, stereo companies, and now high-end adult toy stores like the Sharper Image. There's no denying it: We were spoiled rotten with the toys of our youth, and we're now spoiled as adults. So let's keep playing.

**W**riting this book has been a pleasure because it gave us the opportunity to retrace an important part of our childhoods, but we'd be fooling ourselves if we claimed now to be toy "experts." The photos we found jogged our memories so we could write from personal experience, but we couldn't have finished the text without the real experts in the field—the authors whose books formed a formidable pop-culture research library for us to check facts against and to fill holes in our memories.

Many books proved helpful.

*Great Expectations* by Landon Y. Jones (Ballantine) was, way back in 1980, instrumental in crystallizing the historical force of the American postwar generation. As such, it was an inspiration for our book.

*A. C. Gilbert's Heritage,* edited by Donald J. Heimburger (Heimburger House), offered insights into the A. C. Gilbert Co. by gathering articles and catalogs from over the years. Ron Hollander's indispensable *All Aboard* (Workman) is the last word on Lionel trains. Hollander provided invaluable insights into the rise and decline of model railroading and how the business of selling toys changed during the period.

Philip Orbanes's *The Monopoly Companion* (Bob Adams), although an "official" publication, tells the history of the world's most famous game, or at least, most of it. In the same vein, Cass S. Hough's *It's a Daisy* (Daisy) is mostly exaggerated and self-complimentary public relations hyperbole. Still, it provided an inside look at how a successful company works to keep up with changes in the market over a long period of time.

Another "in-house" book provided by a manufacturer, *Fisher-Price, 1931–1963* (Books Americana), proved half entertaining and informative history, half collector's guide to rarities.

Henry Wiencek's *The World of Lego Toys* (Abrams) is a beautifully designed softcover that explores the best-selling building toy's humble origins and current industry power in awesome detail.

There probably have been more books written about Barbie than about any other single toy in history. Two of them were helpful guides for our date with Barbiemania in the chapter about dolls: Cynthia Robins's slim paperback, *Barbie* (Contemporary Books), and the campy, fun, visually rich, and well-put-together hardback by fashion designer BillyBoy*, *Barbie, Her Life and Times* (Crown). Other doll information was culled from the impressive collector's art book *The Doll* (Harrison House), with text by Carl Fox and photographs by H. Landshoff.

Although we didn't write this book with the stringent requirements of collectors in mind, various published collector's guides were invaluable for their unvarnished factual information, about both specific toys and long-forgotten manufacturers. Crystal and Leland Payton's *Space Toys: A Collector's Guide to Science Fiction and Astronautical Toys* (Collector's Compass) is less a guide to collecting than a rambling yet worthwhile essay on why we're attracted to collecting and the world of science fiction. Likewise, *Greenberg's Guide to Super Hero Toys, Volume I* (Greenberg). Carol Moody's *G.I. Joe Value Guide, 1964–1978* (Hobby House), generously loaned by Eric Rubin, is a straightforward listing of the durable soldier doll's collectibles.

Linda Baker's *Modern American Toys, 1930–1980* (Collector Books) combined evocative studio photos of toys with capsule histories of the companies that created them. For more general information, we often flipped through the informative pages of *The Official Price Guide to Toys* by Richard Fritz, and *The Official Price Guide to Collectibles of the '50s & '60s* by Charles J. Jordan (both published by House of Collectibles).

## BIBLIOGRAPHY

For some of the text covering cars, we turned to *The World of Model Cars* by Guy R. Williams (Rainbird), as well as *Matchbox Toys* by Nancy Schiffer and *Corgi Toys* by Dr. Edward Force (both by Schiffer Publishing).

Arthur Shulman and Roger Youman's 1966 *How Sweet It Was* (Bonanza) aroused incredible old memories with an exhaustive array of 1,435 photographs from television shows between 1950 and 1965. Jefferson Graham's *Come on Down* (Abbeville Press) did the same thing for game shows of the period. Yet another TV book, Harry Castleman and Walter J. Podrazik's *Watching TV* (McGraw-Hill), gave a season-by-season review of programs and their pop impact. The best reference book on television is Tim Brooks and Earle Marsh's truly complete *The Complete Directory to Prime Time Network-TV Shows* (Ballantine).

Jon Heitland's informative *The Man from U.N.C.L.E. Book* (St. Martin's Press) helped spark this book by bringing back the pleasure of the original fad, and including a chapter on the staggering array of licensed toys inspired by the program.

When dates or historical problems came up, we found both *The Timetables of History* (Touchstone) by Bernard Grun, and *American Chronicle: Six Decades in American Life, 1920–1980* (Atheneum) by Lois and Alan Gordon, to be quick and efficient sources for the correct answers.

Although it was a flea-market find, Paul Sann's 1967 *Fads, Follies and Delusions of the American People* (Bonanza) turned out to be a valuable resource for capsule overviews of overnight sensations from Davy Crockett to Super Balls, Hula Hoops to rock 'n' roll (albeit in somewhat deprecating tones). It is, as its subtitle promises, "a pictorial story of madness, crazes and crowd phenomena."

Thomas Hines's *Populuxe* (Alfred A. Knopf) offered a wide-ranging, informative look at life, American style—in fashion, architecture, industrial design, and advertising—during the fifties and sixties.

Andrew J. Edelstein's *The Pop Sixties* (World Almanac Publications) was a heady, mostly irreverent look back at that decade.

And, lest we forget, we occasionally hauled out the heavy tomes of *The World Book* for its articles on everything from "Toys" to "Dolls," and reread the illuminating essays in each annual volume of *The World Book Year Book* from the sixties and early seventies. Opening them to pages with illustrations still fresh after twenty-five years was in itself a cultural epiphany. Never underestimate the value of a good set of encyclopedias.

# Acknowledgments

**F**or inspiration: Frank Kresen, the first person who thought it could be possible; Tim Riley, because without him we never would have had the guts to even try; John Stewart, for first putting the "boomers" in context; Landon Y. Jones, for making sense of our generation; John Heitland, for *The Man from U.N.C.L.E. Book*, which helped convince us that there must be people out there who might read this kind of book (and also for unselfishly sending along his extra copies of Man from U.N.C.L.E. sixties paperbacks); Betty James, who inspired us with her enthusiasm and her continuing commitment to the Slinky.

For the chance: Martha Kaplan, the editor who does "a little of everything"; agent extraordinaire Bob Cornfield; and Marty Asher of Vintage.

For toys: June Sloniger, the Barbie fan who came from nowhere with catalogs for the home stretch; John Silva and Lisa Fancher, rock 'n' rollers with a very large soft spot for sixties bric-a-brac; Linda and Jim Ayres, for holding on to their old toys; Chris McNulty and her cool Melrose shop, Chic-A-Boom; Gail and Mike Thompson of the Antique Trader, the coolest store in Denver.

For the entry into the razzle-dazzle toy industry: the Toy Manufacturers' Association, and communications director Jodi Levin; and every person we contacted at manufacturers around the country, especially David Lewis at Daisy, Kathleen Wade at Lionel, Mark Pasin of Radio Flyer, Barbara Allen of Cadaco, Candace Irving at Mattel, Frank Kappler of Wham-O, Robert Erickson at Merdel Manufacturing, LEGO's team of David LaFrennie and Nancy Tofferi, and Pat Grandy at Ohio Art.

For indispensable help and understanding: Karan Pond, for her computer; Paul Danish, for his printer; *Westword*, the *Colorado Daily,* and Clint Talbott; Dick Kreck, for keeping up with the project in his column; our peers G. Brown, David Menconi, and Justin Mitchell, who've always been there for advice.

For photos: Mrs. Robert H. McConnell, Cheryl Sample, Billie Gutgsell, Asakawas, Eva Schaaf, Barbara Kruck, M. J. Philippus, Ph.D., Shelley Keech, Stephen M. Lee, Charlene Schaaf, Suzanne Frazier. And a special thank-you to Bob Merlis at Warner Bros. Records, who contacted performer Randy Newman for permission to use his terrific childhood portrait on page 67 (he's the cowkid wearing the hat and holding the pistols).

For last-minute fact-checking and making sure we made sense: Joseph Conti, an architect and retired musician; Phil Murray and Terri Dorman, former Vacu-form users; Alan Dumas, a professional know-it-all (especially James Bond stuff); and Kathleen Schaaf, a born proofreader.

For their technical help: editor Susan Ralston, for taking over for the final stretch; production manager Andy Hughes and designer Iris Weinstein, who've explored the brave new world of computer publishing on our behalf, and the rest of the crack editorial/production staff at Knopf; Gary Isaacs, for the studio work; Glenn Asakawa, our California photographer; Dewey Webb of the *Phoenix New Times,* a G.I. Joe expert and awesome pop culture fiend; Eric Rubin, our saving angel who showed us how to reproduce the ads; A-Square Photo and the entire Soricelli clan, who shot stats of much of our art; publisher Harry Guckert, editor Frank Reysen, office manager Aileen Ryan and the staff of *Playthings*, who made much of the book possible; Jerry Robinette's Denver Book Fair, the only place in town for period magazines of all kinds; Ira Gallen, the video keeper of the past, whose Video Resources NY Inc. is a treasure trove of old TV shows and commercials; Ryan Kucera, for her savvy as a

## ACKNOWLEDGMENTS

travel agent for novice jet-setters and her patience digging up old receipts; Ed Pierson, lawyer and friend extraordinaire; Marietta Eckhardt, CPA, for demystifying the process for us.

For one helluva valuable lesson: Officer Dennis Moon of the Denver Police Department, who reminded us of what's real and what's fantasy when we waved around a Mattel Fanner 50 pistol in public.

For laughs: The Partners, for being cost-effective (or so we thought); The Soldiers of Love, for taking a sabbatical; Tommy's Oriental, for iced Thai Coffee; Noah Saunders, for consulting; and Ricky, for being there all the time.

For everything else, and for their support: Billie Gutgsell and Kathi Schaaf.

From Gil: Thanks to George and Junko Asakawa for always spoiling me, and for buying that Man from U.N.C.L.E. trench coat for Christmas 1967; Gary, Pok Sun, and Joann; Glenn and Michelle; Patty Calhoun, for making me a better writer during the ten years I've known and worked for her. And last but not least, thanks to David McCallum—without Illya Kuryakin, I'd never have bought my first turtleneck sweater.

From Leland: Thanks to Harold Dunklau, Howard G. Barth, Ann Waymire, Pet, Vincent, Lena, Garold, Inez and Jack Rucker.

# Index

**A NOTE ABOUT THE AUTHORS**

**LELAND RUCKER** WAS BORN IN KANSAS CITY, MISSOURI, IN 1947, DURING THE FIRST STIRRINGS OF THE BABY BOOM. HIS LIFE WAS IRREVOCABLY CHANGED WHEN HE BECAME THE ONLY KID IN HIS CLASS NOT TO GET A DAVY CROCK-ETT COONSKIN CAP. HE MADE UP FOR IT WITH A VENGEANCE THROUGHOUT THE REST OF THE FIFTIES AND EARLY SIXTIES, WHEN HE COULD BE FOUND PLAYING MONOPOLY OR BASEBALL AT EVERY OPPORTUNITY.

HE RECEIVED A BACHELOR OF ARTS DEGREE IN FOREIGN LANGUAGE AND ENGLISH LITERATURE FROM CONCORDIA SENIOR COLLEGE, FORT WAYNE, INDIANA, AND A TEACHING DEGREE FROM CON-CORDIA TEACHERS COLLEGE, SEWARD, NEBRASKA, IN 1970. AFTER TEACHING JUNIOR HIGH SCHOOL FOR ONE YEAR, HE BECAME

PART OF A FOLK/ROCK MUSIC DUO CALLED THE COALITION FROM 1972 TO 1976. HE STARTED WRITING FOR VARIOUS PUBLICATIONS IN THE KANSAS CITY AREA BEFORE JOIN-ING THE *KANSAS CITY TIMES* IN 1979 AS ROCK CRITIC AND NEWS AND FEATURE WRITER.

HE MOVED TO BOULDER, COLO-RADO, IN 1983, AND HAS BEEN THE ENTERTAINMENT EDITOR OF THE *COLORADO DAILY*, AN ALTER-NATIVE NEWSPAPER GEARED TO THE UNIVERSITY OF COLORADO COMMUNITY, SINCE 1986. HE ALSO WRITES A WEEKLY COLUMN FOR THE *DAILY* ON POPULAR MUSIC AND CULTURE.

**GIL ASAKAWA** WAS BORN AN ARMY BRAT IN JAPAN IN 1957, THE BABY BOOM'S PEAK YEAR, AND HAS SPENT HIS LIFE TRYING TO STICK OUT IN THE CROWD. HE WAS SPOILED ROTTEN FROM THE START, AND SPENT HIS YOUTH ALTERNA-TIVELY DRESSED AS A COWBOY AND A SAMURAI. IN 1966, HIS FAMILY MOVED TO THE UNITED STATES, WHERE HE WAS ENTRANCED BY "THE MAN FROM U.N.C.L.E." THAT CHRISTMAS, HE THREATENED TO RUN AWAY FROM HOME UNLESS HIS PARENTS BOUGHT HIM AN U.N.C.L.E. TRENCH COAT, AND HE PROMPTLY WORE IT TO TATTERS. HE ATTENDED PRATT INSTITUTE IN NEW YORK CITY AND GRADUATED IN 1979 WITH A BACHELOR OF FINE ARTS IN PAINTING. HE STARTED HIS WRITING CAREER AS AN ART CRITIC AND MUSIC WRITER IN BOULDER FOR THE *COLORADO DAILY*, AND IN 1980 BECAME THE CHIEF ROCK CRITIC FOR *WESTWORD*, DENVER'S ALTERNATIVE WEEKLY NEWSPAPER.

HE WAS FULL-TIME MUSIC EDITOR AND REPORTER THERE FROM 1983 TO 1990. HE IS CURRENTLY A FREELANCE WRITER FOR *ROLLING STONE, CREEM*, AND OTHER PUBLI-CATIONS, AND WRITES AN AMERI-CAN ROCK COLUMN FOR *KOMSOMOLSKAYA PRAVDA*, RUS-SIA'S LARGEST-CIRCULATION DAILY PAPER. HE STILL SCANS CABLE LISTINGS FOR "U.N.C.L.E." RERUNS, AND CAN OCCASIONALLY BE SEEN FURTIVELY WHISPERING INTO A PEN, "OPEN CHAN-NEL D."

THE AUTHORS MET IN 1983 WHEN ASAKAWA TURNED RUCKER DOWN FOR A WRITING POSITION. THEY LATER DISCOVERED THEY HAD SIMI-LAR TASTES IN MUSIC, AND HAVE BEEN CLOSE FRIENDS SINCE. THE TWO HOSTED A PROGRAM ON LOCAL PUBLIC RADIO FOR A YEAR, "AT THE TURNTABLES," ON WHICH THEY REVIEWED, ARGUED OVER, AND GENERALLY BERATED EACH OTHER ABOUT THE LATEST RECORDINGS. THEY ALSO PERFORM TOGETHER AS THE SOLDIERS OF LOVE, A ROCK/PUNK/FOLK DUO WITH ACOUSTIC GUITARS THAT PLAYS ON BOULDER'S OUTDOOR PEARL STREET MALL WHENEVER WEATHER PERMITS.

## A NOTE ON THE TYPE

THE TEXT OF THIS BOOK WAS CREATED IN A DIGITIZED VERSION OF SOUVENIR, A TYPEFACE ORIGINALLY DRAWN BY MORRIS FULLER BENTON IN 1914 FOR AMERICAN TYPE FOUNDERS. WITH ITS EASY, OPEN CURVES AND ITS GENTLE FLOWING QUALITY, SOUVENIR HAS BEEN WIDELY ACCEPTED AS ONE OF THE FINEST AND MOST USEFUL CONTRIBUTIONS TO CONTEMPORARY TYPE DESIGN.

THE MANUSCRIPT WAS PREPARED IN MICROSOFT WORD, AND COPY WAS IMPORTED TO QUARK XPRESS™, WHERE ORIGINAL DUMMIES AND FINAL LAYOUTS WERE GENERATED. IMAGES WERE ELECTRONICALLY CAPTURED USING A XEROX 7650 FLATBED SCANNER. COLORIZATION, RETOUCHING, AND SILHOUETTING WERE DONE IN ADOBE PHOTOSHOP. THE PAGINATION WAS DONE ON A MACINTOSH IIFX, WITH EIGHT MEGABYTES OF RAM AND OVER TWO GIGABYTES OF HARD STORAGE. FINAL SEPARATED POSITIVES WERE IMAGE SET ON AN AGFA 9800 AT 133 LINES PER INCH.

COMPOSITION, IMAGE SCANNING, COLORIZATION, AND RETOUCHING WIZARDRY BY PAUL MURRAY AND LAURA HICKMAN AT NORTH MARKET STREET GRAPHICS, LANCASTER, PENNSYLVANIA

PRINTING AND BINDING SUPERVISED BY MARTIN COOK ASSOCIATES, LTD., NEW YORK, NEW YORK

ELECTRONICS PRODUCED BY IDEATECH INDUSTRIAL, LTD., KOWLOON, HONG KONG

ASSEMBLED BY WIDE SKILL INDUSTRIAL, LTD., SHANG NAN, CHINA

MANUFACTURING DIRECTED BY ANDREW N. HUGHES

BOOK DESIGN BY IRIS WEINSTEIN